SpringerBriefs in Sociology

More information about this series at http://www.springer.com/series/10410

Giulia Maria Dotti Sani

Time Use in Domestic Settings Throughout the Life Course

The Italian Case

Giulia Maria Dotti Sani
European University Institute
San Domenico di Fiesole
Italy

ISSN 2212-6368 ISSN 2212-6376 (electronic)
SpringerBriefs in Sociology
ISBN 978-3-319-78719-0 ISBN 978-3-319-78720-6 (eBook)
https://doi.org/10.1007/978-3-319-78720-6

Library of Congress Control Number: 2018936637

© The Author(s) 2018
This work is subject to copyright. All rights are reserved by the Publisher, whether the whole or part of the material is concerned, specifically the rights of translation, reprinting, reuse of illustrations, recitation, broadcasting, reproduction on microfilms or in any other physical way, and transmission or information storage and retrieval, electronic adaptation, computer software, or by similar or dissimilar methodology now known or hereafter developed.
The use of general descriptive names, registered names, trademarks, service marks, etc. in this publication does not imply, even in the absence of a specific statement, that such names are exempt from the relevant protective laws and regulations and therefore free for general use.
The publisher, the authors and the editors are safe to assume that the advice and information in this book are believed to be true and accurate at the date of publication. Neither the publisher nor the authors or the editors give a warranty, express or implied, with respect to the material contained herein or for any errors or omissions that may have been made. The publisher remains neutral with regard to jurisdictional claims in published maps and institutional affiliations.

Printed on acid-free paper

This Springer imprint is published by the registered company Springer International Publishing AG part of Springer Nature
The registered company address is: Gewerbestrasse 11, 6330 Cham, Switzerland

To Alice and Cecilia

Acknowledgements

This book would not have seen the light of day without the help, support, insights, comments, constructive criticisms and suggestions of many people. I finally have the opportunity to thank them, and I do so with immense pleasure.

First of all, I would like to express my gratitude to two professors whose work I greatly admire: Judith Treas and Tiziana Nazio. Thank you for your ongoing support during my academic path and for setting the bar so high.

I am extremely thankful to the three anonymous referees whose invaluable suggestions immensely contributed to the development of the volume from book proposal to finished manuscript.

I would also like to thank the Max Weber Programme at the European University Institute, which provided an ideal academic environment to conclude this endeavour; in particular, Nevena Kulic for her invitation to present the volume at the Max Weber Multidisciplinary Workshop: Persistent Inequalities: Studying Gender in the 21st Century; Laurie Anderson and Alyson Price for their careful and attentive reading that helped me immensely in the final, polishing-off stage of the writing.

I am also indebted to the researchers and staff at the ADELE laboratory of Milano, as well as ISTAT for providing such a wealth of data.

A special thank you goes to my colleagues and fellows at the Collegio Carlo Alberto, who have been a continuous intellectual stimulus for my work over the past years; above all my colleagues Nicole Scicluna, Moreno Mancosu and Matteo Luppi for endless conversations and debates about those things we call politics and society; and Stefano Sacchi and Margarita Estevez-Abe for providing an excellent environment for independent academic research.

Beyond academia, thank you Giulia and Moreno for listening to me go on and on about the book, be it during the commute on the 9900 train, endless vocal messages, or our double date nights out. Simply, thank you for your friendship.

Thanks to Marina, Gabriella, Carla and Stefano for their patience, emotional support, company and childcare during the family holidays I spent writing.

Thanks to my mother, my role model, for dressing me like a witch and not like a princess on Halloween and for giving up on the ballet class in favour of martial arts. Thanks to my father, who I wish were still with us.

Thanks to Alice, who enjoys playing with brooms and dustpans, but also with cars and footballs, and hopefully will never be asked to choose one over the other. Thank you, Cecilia, for joining us.

Finally, thanks to Mario, for reading, revising, re-reading and re-revising. Thank you for your suggestions, thoughts, insights. But most of all, thank you for equally sharing with me the cooking, the cleaning and the washing, the laundry, the shopping, the diaper changing and the baby feeding, the late-night crying and the stroller pushing, the storytelling and lullaby singing.

Contents

1 **Introduction** 1
   1.1 Domestic Work Over the Life Course 1
   1.2 Italy: A Case of Lowest-Low Gender Equality 2
   1.3 The Life Course Approach 3
   1.4 Research Questions and Structure of the Book 4
   References 7

2 **Theoretical Background** 11
   2.1 Gender Inequalities in Domestic Work: An Overview 11
   2.2 The Micro- and Macro-Determinants of Housework 13
   2.3 Theoretical Accounts for Time Spent on Childcare
        and Adult Care 16
   2.4 Explaining Housework Among Children, Adolescents
        and Young Adults 18
   2.5 Conclusions 20
   References 21

3 **The Italian Time Use Survey** 27
   3.1 Time Use Data: What Is It and How Can We Use It? 27
   3.2 The Italian Time Use Survey 28
   3.3 Gauging the Life Cycle: Respondents Age-Groups 30
   3.4 Analysing Housework, Childcare and Adult Care 31
       3.4.1 Measures 31
       3.4.2 Analyses 32
       3.4.3 Independent Variables 33
   3.5 Housework, Childcare and Adult Care Over the Life Course 34
       3.5.1 Housework 34
       3.5.2 Childcare 40
       3.5.3 Adult Care 44

		3.6 Conclusions	45
		References	47
4	**Domestic Work Among Children, Teenagers, and Young Adults**		49
	4.1	Introduction	49
	4.2	Children's Housework Time and Participation: Who Is Doing What?	50
	4.3	The Correlates of Children's Housework: Family Structure, Parental Education, Working Status and Housework Participation	52
	4.4	Conclusions	61
		References	63
5	**Young and Beautiful. Domestic Work Among Childless Women and Men**		65
	5.1	Introduction	65
	5.2	Housework Among Childless Couples: Who Is Doing What?	66
	5.3	Determinants of Housework Among Childless Young Adults: What Matters?	69
	5.4	Conclusions	77
		References	77
6	**Parenthood and Domestic Work: A Never-Ending Workload**		79
	6.1	Introduction	79
	6.2	Parents' Time on Housework	80
	6.3	Childcare and Adult Care	90
	6.4	Conclusions	100
		References	101
7	**When the Kids Grow up: Domestic Work Among Italians Aged 45–64**		103
	7.1	Introduction	103
	7.2	Housework Time Among Mature Couples: Growing Differences Between Women and Men?	104
	7.3	Emerging Care Needs from Frail Family Members	114
	7.4	Conclusions	115
		References	115
8	**In the Empty Nest: Housework and Adult Care Among Italians Aged 65 and Above**		117
	8.1	Introduction	117
	8.2	Housework Among Elder Adults	118
	8.3	Division of Domestic Work Among Older Adults	125

	8.4	Adult Care in the Empty Nest	127
	8.5	Conclusions	128
		References	130
9	**Conclusions**	131
	9.1	Time Use in the Domestic Setting in Italy: Essential Facts and Figures	131
	9.2	Traditional Behaviours, Traditional Attitudes?	134
	9.3	Changing Times: Historical Changes in Housework and Childcare	137
	9.4	Concluding Remarks	140
		References	141

About the Author

Giulia Maria Dotti Sani is a Max Weber Fellow at the European University Institute, Florence. She holds a Ph.D. in Sociology and Social Research from the University of Trento. Her main research areas are sociology of the family, female employment and social stratification. Her methodological skills include time budget analysis, multilevel and panel modelling. She is specialized in the management and analyses of large household longitudinal and cross-sectional data sets (e.g. EU-SILC, ESS, ISTAT Household Survey) and has several years of teaching experience in quantitative methods at the master and Ph.D. levels. She also has an interest in the making of political inequalities within and between European households and in the relation between social and political inequalities. Her work has appeared in international peer-reviewed journals such as the *European Sociological Review*, the *Journal of Marriage and Family*, *Sex Roles* and the *European Journal of Political Research*.

Chapter 1
Introduction

Abstract This is an introductory chapter that provides an overview of the motivation for the volume, a presentation of the case used in the study, Italy, a description of the objectives and research questions and the contents of each chapter. The chapter discusses the importance of studying the allocation of time to the domestic sphere in a context of low gender equality and explains why the life course approach adopted in the volume can provide valuable insights to our understanding of inequalities in housework, childcare and adult care in Italy.

Keywords Domestic work · Housework · Childcare · Adult care
Life course · Italy · Italian time use survey · Gender inequality

1.1 Domestic Work Over the Life Course

Recent evidence suggests that, worldwide, women's days are considerably more frantic than men's. While men spend more time than women doing *paid* work, women spend more time working than men when both *unpaid and paid* activities are considered (World Economic Forum, WEF 2016). This gender gap emerges because the allocation of time to domestic work remains largely gender unequal, despite women's advances in Western and non-Western societies over the past decades (Altintas and Sullivan 2016; Bianchi et al. 2000, 2014; Dotti Sani 2014; Geist and Cohen 2011; Geist 2005; Hook 2006, 2010; Knudsen and Wærness 2008). In many countries, the overrepresentation of women in the private sphere translates into a diminished presence in the public sphere, with inevitable consequences in terms of gender inequality in employment (OECD 2016), earnings (Bryan and Sevilla-Sanz 2011) and political representation (Inter Parliamentary Union, IPU 2014). However, while women have come closer to achieving gender equality in the allocation of time to the private and public sphere in some countries, in others they still retain the lions' share of unpaid domestic labour as well as a marginal position in the public sphere. In this volume, I analyse one of these countries, infamous for its gender-unequal division of household labour: Italy. The

© The Author(s) 2018
G. M. Dotti Sani, *Time Use in Domestic Settings Throughout the Life Course*,
SpringerBriefs in Sociology, https://doi.org/10.1007/978-3-319-78720-6_1

aim of the book is to provide a comprehensive, coherent and systematic overview of the three cornerstones of domestic work—housework, childcare and adult care—in this country.

Spurred by a growing recognition of the importance of an equal division of domestic work between women and men to achieve broader societal gender equality, studies on domestic work have flourished cross-nationally over the past decades. This body of research has provided much needed cross-sectional and longitudinal evidence on the distribution of housework (Bianchi et al. 2012, 2014; Dotti Sani 2014; Hook 2010), childcare (Craig and Mullan 2011; Dotti Sani and Treas 2016; England and Srivastava 2013; Gauthier et al. 2004) and to a smaller extent adult care (Chesley and Poppie 2009; Henz 2010; Sarkisian and Gerstel 2004). Research has also shed light on the determinants of time spent on and participation in domestic work, revealing the importance of individual factors such as time availability (Blood and Wolfe 1960; Presser 1994), economic resources (Bittman et al. 2003; Brines 1994; Treas and De Ruijter 2008), and gender ideology (West and Zimmerman 1987, 2009); contextual characteristics like female labour force participation, gender empowerment and standard work hours have also received attention (Dotti Sani 2014; Fuwa 2004; Hook 2006). However, empirical evidence is concentrated in the US (Bianchi 2011; England and Srivastava 2013; Treas and De Ruijter 2008; Wight et al. 2009 among others), some European countries such as the UK, Denmark, Spain and the Netherlands (Bianchi et al. 2014; Bonke 2010; Bryan and Sevilla-Sanz 2011; Burt and Scott 2002; Craig and Mullan 2011; Poortman and Van der Lippe 2009) and Australia (Baxter et al. 2008; Craig et al. 2015). With few exceptions (see Bianchi et al. 2014; Carriero and Todesco 2011, 2016; Carriero 2009; Dotti Sani 2012, 2016), less is known about housework, childcare and adult care among Italian women and men. Moreover, most studies have focused on adults of working age, while only a marginal part of the literature is centred on other stages of the life course. As will be discussed in the following sections, studying individuals in different points of the life course can contribute very meaningful insights to our scientific understanding of gender disparities in domestic work.

1.2 Italy: A Case of Lowest-Low Gender Equality

Italy represents an extraordinary case for the analysis of the gendered allocation of time to unpaid domestic work, as it is among the European Union countries with the lowest levels of societal gender equality, according to the Gender Equality Index[1] (EIGE 2015). The inequality of the Italian context gauged by this index involves

---

[1]The Gender Equality Index is an indicator that provides a composite measure of gender equality in EU member countries. It measures gaps between women and men in various areas such as work, money, knowledge, time, power, health, violence and intersecting inequalities (www.eige.europa.eu/gender-statistics).

multiple areas. For example, although female labour force participation has increased over recent decades, from 38.7% in 1993 to 51.6% in 2016 (Eurostat 2017), women are still much more likely to be full-time homemakers in Italy than in other European countries (Bettio et al. 2013; Dotti Sani and Scherer 2017; Eurostat 2017; OECD 2017). More important to the central theme of this book, research shows that responsibility for unpaid domestic labour falls disproportionately on the shoulders of women (Anxo et al. 2011; Carriero and Todesco 2016) even among dual-earner couples (Dotti Sani 2012). Exploiting the strong family ties that characterize Italian society (Dalla Zuanna 2001), the Italian welfare state largely relies on the ability of Italian families to provide for their own care needs (Saraceno 1994), forcing women to shoulder family responsibilities that in other countries can be offloaded to the state or the market (Esping-Andersen 2009).>

A paucity of women in the Italian political sphere (IPU 2014) is often invoked to account for the lack of policies and services that could facilitate the reconciliation of work and family. Values and norms concerning the position and roles of women and men in society also come into play. According to the European Values Study (EVS), Italians have more traditional attitudes regarding gender roles compared to citizens of other European countries. For example, more than 60% of Italian women and men aged 18–65 in 2008 agreed with the statement "what women really want is home and children" as opposed to 49% in Portugal, 41% in Spain, and 32% in Norway (EVS 2011).[2] Italy is also characterised by rather traditional behaviours regarding family formation. It is among the OECD countries with the lowest divorce rates (albeit on the rise): less than 1‰ in 2014 compared to 3.2‰ in the US and 3.4‰ Denmark and an OECD average of 2.1‰. Moreover, as of 2014, cohabitation is much rarer than in other countries (OECD 2017) and just about 28.8% of births occur out of marriage, fewer than the OECD average (39.9%) and than in other continental European countries such as Germany (35%) and Spain (42.5%). Studying the allocation of time to housework, childcare and adult care in this context is imperative to achieve a better understanding of the production and reproduction of gender inequalities.

1.3 The Life Course Approach

Previous research has provided important insights into inequalities in domestic work in Italy (Bianchi et al. 2014; Carriero and Todesco 2011, 2016; Carriero 2009; Dotti Sani 2012, 2016). Compared to other countries, however, research has focused mainly on working age women and men, while little is known about the allocation of time to domestic work in other stages of the life course.

Why is it essential to go beyond the study of household labour among working age individuals?

---

[2]Own calculation.

To begin with, understanding the allocation of time to and participation in housework among children and adolescents is important because it provides insights into the *socialization* to gender roles in housework that may affect the later division of domestic chores (Bandura 1977). Similarly, focusing on domestic work among childless young women and men living independently vis-a-vis in couples can shed light on the allocation of housework under different configurations of time, power, resources and preferences (Blood and Wolfe 1960; Brines 1994; West and Zimmerman 1987, 2009).

Moreover, few studies have focused on parents of children of different ages when analysing housework and childcare time and its division among Italian mothers and fathers, despite the fact that several studies have shown that the transition to parenthood strongly affects gender inequality in housework and that the amount of time parents spend on housework and childcare and how they share it is highly affected by the presence and age of children (Baxter et al. 2008; Naldini and Torrioni 2015; Schober 2013). Therefore, it appears fruitful to compare parents of children in different age groups in order to better understand gender-unequal behaviour over the life course.

Finally, focusing on Italians in later stages of the life course is pivotal because individuals age 65 and older are becoming an increasingly large portion of the population. These subjects also act as role models to which Italian youth look up at and imitate, thus potentially reinforcing existing patterns of gendered behaviour. Older adults are also likely to be involved in the care of other adults, such as a parent or a spouse. The study of subjects in later stages of the life course is therefore likely to unveil important aspects regarding the allocation of time to the "third pillar" of domestic work: adult care.

1.4 Research Questions and Structure of the Book

The volume adds to the existing literature on unpaid household labour by offering a comprehensive overview of time spent on and participation in domestic work—that is, housework, childcare and adult care—over the life course in Italy. In it, univariate, bivariate and multivariate analyses are applied to four waves of data from the nationally representative Italian Time Use Survey (ISTAT 1988–1989, 2002–2003, 2008–2009, 2013–2014) to address five sets of research questions:

  i. How much time do Italians spend in housework, childcare and adult care over the life course? What activities take up more time at different life stages? Do women and men at different ages engage in different activities? How much has the distribution of domestic work changed since the first wave of Italian time use data in the late '80s?
 ii. What is the allocation of time to housework and participation in domestic chores among Italian children, teenagers and young adults living in the parental home? Do gendered patterns of housework emerge already at this stage?

1.4 Research Questions and Structure of the Book

Do children learn how to "do gender" in housework by following their parents' example?

iii. How do childless Italian adults living on their own or in couples allocate time to housework? What is the link between individual characteristics and domestic work? What gendered patterns of behaviour appear in this age group, which is likely to be less affected by time and resource constraints compared to parents and older adults? In couples, do individual level resources, such as education and relative income, mediate the way partners share housework?

iv. Parents are known to spend more time on domestic work than childless women and men. Children of different ages, however, have different needs and demands and are likely to take a different toll on their parents' time. How much does the presence in the home of children of different ages affect mothers' and fathers' domestic work? To what extent do parents' individual characteristics, such as level of education and employment status, interact with the presence of children of different ages? How much time do parents of younger and older children spend on adult care?

v. How much time do Italians aged 65 and above spend on housework? How do elderly couples share domestic chores? How much time do adults above 65 spend taking care of an older parent or an ageing spouse?

Eight chapters address these questions. The second chapter ("Theoretical background") represents the theoretical backbone of the volume. It provides a review of the extant studies on housework, childcare and adult care in Italy and internationally. Moreover, it describes the dominant theories that have been used to explain the allocation of time on and participation in domestic chores by women and men, namely time availability, relative resources and gender ideology. Furthermore, the chapter provides an overview of the literature regarding childcare, which is close to the literature on housework but has some very distinct features. The chapter also discusses previous findings regarding the understudied topic of time spent providing care to other adults, usually elderly parents or spouses. Finally, it provides a review of the literature on housework time and participation among children, teenagers and young adults. This topic is treated in a separate section because explanations based on time availability and resources do not fully account for young peoples' time on domestic work. Indeed, housework time in this age group is affected by other factors that require an ad hoc discussion.

Chapter 3 ("The Italian Time Use Survey") illustrates the dataset used throughout the volume: the Italian Time Use Survey (TUS) for the periods 1988–1989, 2002–2003, 2008–2009 and 2013–2014. Over the last few decades, these data collected by the Italian National Institute for Statistics (ISTAT) have been a superior source of information on how Italians spend their days and nights. By relying on daily diaries rather than reports of time spent on given activities, the Italian TUS allows reaching very precise and detailed estimates of time use. Moreover, the data are available at the household level, thus allowing researchers to go beyond the study of individuals and focus on the interplay of mothers, fathers, daughters and sons. Chapter three also describes the main measures and techniques used in the volume. Substantially, the chapter provides descriptive evidence of time allocated to and participation in overall housework at different stages of the life course. Various childcare activities are also discussed. Finally, the chapter provides descriptive statistics on time on and participation in adult care.

The following chapters engage with more comprehensive, nuanced and detailed analyses of housework, childcare and adult care. Specifically, each chapter focuses on a specific stage of the life course, exploring what individual and household characteristics are associated with time on and participation in domestic work. The chapters follow the order of the life course, starting from children and ending with adults aged 65 and older.

The fourth chapter ("Domestic work among children, teenagers and young adults") focuses on an often neglected aspect in time use studies, that is, domestic work among sons and daughters. The chapter goes beyond descriptive evidence of the time children of different ages spend on the various components of housework by looking at how the characteristics of children and their parents matter for participation in domestic chores. In particular, the chapter provides empirical evidence of a gender gap in housework among children, teenagers and young adults. Moreover, it shows that gender differences in housework participation become wider as children grow older due to an increase of daughters' but not sons' participation. This finding indicates that adherence to traditional gender roles is rooted in childhood and reinforced throughout adolescence up to early adulthood.

Chapter 5 ("Young and beautiful: domestic work among childless women and men") focuses on the allocation of time to housework among Italian women and men who have left the parental home and are either living on their own or in couples. Drawing on theories of relative resources, time availability and gender ideology, the chapter demonstrates how young women and men with specific characteristics—in terms of age, level of education or working status—spend different amounts of time on housework. The chapter also provides empirical evidence of the division of domestic chores between partners by focusing on the relative rather than the absolute time spent on housework.

Chapter 6 ("Parenthood and domestic work: a never-ending workload") illustrates the amount of time spent on domestic work by mothers and fathers whose children are 14 or younger. Specifically, it elaborates on the individual correlates of housework and childcare time for both mothers and fathers, answering questions about what individual characteristics are more relevant in explaining parents' time on housework and childcare when preschool, primary or lower secondary school children are present. Theories on class differentiation are called upon to explain differences in the time parents spend on childcare. Furthermore, the chapter analyses the allocation of time to adult care among parents.

Chapter 7 ("When the kids grow up: domestic work among Italians aged 45–64") explores the determinants of time spent on housework and other domestic work among parents of children aged 15 and above and subjects between 45 and 64 years old who are childless or whose children have left the parental home. This phase is especially interesting because, while the requirements related to the domestic sphere should become less demanding as compared to when young children are present, ulterior care needs may emerge from other aging family members.

Finally, Chap. 8 ("In the empty nest: housework and adult care among Italians aged 65 and above") focuses on another neglected aspect in the study of domestic work, that is, housework time and participation among elderly women and men. By focusing on elder women and men rather than on working age subjects, the chapter provides fresh insights into the embeddedness of norms regulating the division of chores in a context of low gender equality. Moreover, the chapter explores a further area of caregiving, that is, care provided to an ageing partner or a very old parent.

The final chapter ("Conclusions") summarizes the main findings of the volume. It also exploits the repeated wave design of the data to provide empirical evidence on the historical changes in women's and men's housework and childcare time from the late 1980s to 2013–2014. Moreover, it explores links between the results of the analysis and attitudinal data from the same respondents which reveal a surprisingly high level of satisfaction toward the division of household labour. Finally, the chapter underlines the relevance of the topic for the research community and the broader public and points out directions for future research.

References

Altintas, E., & Sullivan, O. (2016). Fifty years of change updated: Cross-national gender convergence in housework. *Demographic Research, 35,* 455.

Anxo, D., Mencarini, L., Pailhé, A., Solaz, A., et al. (2011). Gender differences in time use over the life course in France, Italy, Sweden, and the US. *Feminist Economics, 17*(3), 159–195.

Bandura, A. (1977). *Social learning theory.* Oxford, England: Prentice-Hall.

Baxter, J., Hewitt, B., & Haynes, M. (2008). Life course transitions and housework: Marriage, parenthood, and time on housework. *Journal of Marriage and Family, 70*(2), 259–272.

Bettio, F., Plantenga, J., & Smith, M. (Eds.). (2013). *Gender and the European labour market.* London: Routledge.

Bianchi, S., Lesnard, L., Nazio, T., & Raley, S. (2014). Gender and time allocation of cohabiting and married women and men in France, Italy, and the United States. *Demographic Research, 31*(8), 183–216.

Bianchi, S., Milkie, M., Sayer, L., & Robinson, J. (2000). Is anyone doing the housework? Trends in the gender division of household labor. *Social Forces, 79*(1), 191–228.

Bianchi, S. M. (2011). Family change and time allocation in American families. *The ANNALS of the American Academy of Political and Social Science, 638*(1), 21–44.

Bianchi, S. M., Sayer, L. C., Milkie, M. A., & Robinson, J. P. (2012). Housework: Who did, does or will do it, and how much does it matter? *Social Forces, 91*(1), 55–63.

Bittman, M., England, P., Sayer, L., Folbre, N., et al. (2003). When does gender trump money? Bargaining and time in household work. *American Journal of Sociology, 109*(1), 186–214.

Blood, R., & Wolfe, D. (1960). *Husbands and wives: The dynamics of married living.* New York, NY: Free Press.

Bonke, J. (2010). Children's housework-Are girls more active than boys? *Electronic International Journal of Time Use Research, 7*(1), 1–16.

Brines, J. (1994). Economic dependency, gender, and the division of labor at home. *American Journal of Sociology, 100*(3), 652–688.

Bryan, M. L., & Sevilla-Sanz, A. (2011). Does housework lower wages? Evidence for Britain. *Oxford Economic Papers, 63*(1), 187–210.

Burt, K. B., & Scott, J. (2002). Parent and adolescent gender role attitudes in 1990s Great Britain. *Sex Roles, 46*(7–8), 239–245.

Carriero, R. (2009). A ciascuno il suo compito. Modelli di divisione del lavoro nella coppia in realtà metropolitane. *Stato e mercato, 87*(3), 421–450.

Carriero, R., & Todesco, L. (2011). La divisione del lavoro domestico: l'esempio dei genitori conta? Uno studio a Torino. *Polis, 25*(1), 37–64.

Carriero, R., & Todesco, L. (2016). *Indaffarate e soddisfatte. Donne, uomini e lavoro familiare in Italia*. Rome: Carocci Editore.

Chesley, N., & Poppie, K. (2009). Assisting parents and in-laws: Gender, type of assistance, and couples' employment. *Journal of Marriage and Family, 71*(2), 247–262.

Craig, L., & Mullan, K. (2011). How mothers and fathers share childcare a cross-national time-use comparison. *American Sociological Review, 76*(6), 834–861.

Craig, L., Powell, A., & Brown, J. E. (2015). Co-resident parents and young people aged 15–34: Who does what housework? *Social Indicators Research, 121*(2), 569–588.

Dalla Zuanna, G. (2001). The banquet of Aeolus: A familistic interpretation of Italy's lowest low fertility. *Demographic Research, 4*(5), 133–162.

Dotti Sani, G. M. (2012). La divisione del lavoro domestico e delle attività di cura nelle coppie italiane: un'analisi empirica. *Stato e Mercato, 94*(1), 161–192.

Dotti Sani, G. M. (2014). Men's employment hours and time on domestic chores in European countries. *Journal of Family Issues, 35*(8), 1023–1047.

Dotti Sani, G. M. (2016). Undoing gender in housework? Participation in domestic chores by Italian fathers and children of different ages. *Sex Roles, 74*(9–10), 411–421.

Dotti Sani, G. M., & Scherer, S. (2017). Maternal employment: Enabling factors in context. First published January 2017. *Work, Employment and Society*, 1–18.

Dotti Sani, G. M., & Treas, J. (2016). Educational gradients in parents' child-care time across countries, 1965–2012. *Journal of Marriage and Family, 78*(4), 1083–1096.

EIGE. (2015). *Gender Equality Index 2015. European Institute for Gender Equality*. www.eige.europa.eu/gender-statistics.

England, P., & Srivastava, A. (2013). Educational differences in US parents' time spent in child care: The role of culture and cross-spouse influence. *Social Science Research, 42*(4), 971–988.

Esping-Andersen, G. (2009). *The incomplete revolution: Adapting to women's new roles*. Cambridge: Polity.

Eurostat. (2017). *Employment, main characteristics and rates. Annual averages*. Retrieved July 7, 2017, from http://appsso.eurostat.ec.europa.eu/nui/submitViewTableAction.do.

EVS. (2011). *European values study longitudinal data file 1981–2008 (EVS 1981–2008)*. GESIS Data Archive, Cologne. ZA4804 Data file Version 2.0.0.

Fuwa, M. (2004). Macro-level gender inequality and the division of household labor in 22 countries. *American Sociological Review, 69*(6), 751–767.

Gauthier, A. H., Smeeding, T. M., & Furstenberg, F. F. (2004). Are parents investing less time in children? Trends in selected industrialized countries. *Population and Development Review, 30*(4), 647–672.

Geist, C. (2005). The welfare state and the home: Regime differences in the domestic division of labour. *European Sociological Review, 21*(1), 23–41.

Geist, C., & Cohen, P. N. (2011). Headed toward equality? Housework change in comparative perspective. *Journal of Marriage and Family, 73*(4), 832–844.

Henz, U. (2010). Parent care as unpaid family labor: How do spouses share? *Journal of Marriage and Family, 72*(1), 148–164.

Hook, J. L. (2006). Care in context: Men's unpaid work in 20 countries, 1965–2003. *American Sociological Review, 71*(4), 639–660.

Hook, J. L. (2010). Gender inequality in the welfare state: Sex segregation in housework, 1965–2003. *American Journal of Sociology, 115*(5), 1480–1523.

References

IPU. (2014). *Women in national parliaments*. Retrieved Oct 7, 2016, from http://www.ipu.org/isse/women.htm.

ISTAT. (1988). *Indagine Multiscopo sulle Famiglie. Uso del Tempo Anno 1988–1989*.

ISTAT. (2002). *Indagine Multiscopo sulle Famiglie. Uso del Tempo Anno 2002–2003*.

ISTAT. (2008). *Indagine Multiscopo sulle Famiglie. Uso del Tempo Anno 2008–2009*.

ISTAT. (2013). *Indagine Multiscopo sulle Famiglie. Uso del Tempo Anno 2013–2014*.

Knudsen, K., & Wærness, K. (2008). National context and spouses' housework in 34 countries. *European Sociological Review, 24*(1), 97–113.

Naldini, M., & Torrioni, P. M. (2015). Una rivoluzione ancora in stallo? La divisione del lavoro domestico e di cura prima e dopo la nascita. In Naldini, M. (Ed.) *La transizione alla genitorialità*. Bologna: Il Mulino.

OECD. (2016.) *LMF1.6: Gender differences in employment outcomes.* Retrieved August 8, 2017.

OECD. (2017). *OECD Family Database*. Retrieved October 26, 2016.

Poortman, A. R., & Van der Lippe, T. (2009). Attitudes toward housework and child care and the gendered division of labor. *Journal of Marriage and Family, 71*(3), 526–541.

Presser, H. B. (1994). Employment schedules among dual-earner spouses and the division of household labor by gender. *American Sociological Review*, 348–64.

Saraceno, C. (1994). The ambivalent familism of the Italian welfare state. *Social Politics, 1*(1), 60–82.

Sarkisian, N., & Gerstel, N. (2004). Explaining the gender gap in help to parents: The importance of employment. *Journal of Marriage and Family., 66*(2), 431–451.

Schober, P. S. (2013). The parenthood effect on gender inequality: Explaining the change in paid and domestic work when British couples become parents. *European Sociological Review, 29*(1), 74–85.

Treas, J., & De Ruijter, E. (2008). Earnings and expenditures on household services in married and cohabiting unions. *Journal of Marriage and Family, 70*(3), 796–805.

WEF. (2016). *The Global Gender Gap Report*. World Economic Forum, Geneva, Switzerland. http://reports.weforum.org/global-gender-gap-report-2016.

West, C., & Zimmerman, D. (1987). Doing gender. *Gender and Society, 1*(2), 125–151.

West, C., & Zimmerman, D. (2009). Accounting for doing gender. *Gender and Society, 23*(1), 112–122.

Wight, V. R., Price, J., Bianchi, S. M., & Hunt, B. R. (2009). The time use of teenagers. *Social Science Research, 38*(4), 792–809.

Chapter 2
Theoretical Background

Abstract This chapter is the theoretical backbone of the volume, offering a comprehensive overview of the theories and literature concerning the three cornerstones of domestic work: housework, childcare and adult care. The chapter provides a broad overview of gender inequalities in domestic work and engages in a detailed review of the literature on the micro and macro determinants of housework in Italy and internationally. Theories of time availability, gender ideology and relative resources are discussed and then used throughout the volume to guide the interpretation of the findings. The chapter also engages with the theoretical accounts for time spent on childcare, in particular regarding intensive parenting styles and concerted cultivation. Finally, the chapter discusses time on adult care and its correlates, and provides a specific literature review about the determinants of housework time and participation among children, teenagers and young adults.

Keywords Relative resources · Time availability · Gender ideology
Domestic work · Housework · Childcare · Adult care

2.1 Gender Inequalities in Domestic Work: An Overview

All prior research shows that, up to the present, women invest significantly more time in unpaid domestic work compared to their male counterparts. Despite the narrowing of gender differences in the public sphere in recent years (Eurostat 2017), the empirical literature agrees that the division of labour inside households is still strongly gender unequal (Dotti Sani 2014; Geist and Cohen 2011; Treas and Tai 2016), even when women are employed (Dotti Sani 2012) and earn more than their partner (Schneider 2011). When it comes to the question "who is doing the housework?" the answer is still: women. Cross-national evidence indicates that, worldwide, women spend more time on housework than men (Gershuny 2000; Treas and Drobnič 2010) and that housework is not shared equally between partners (Dotti Sani 2014; Knudsen and Wærness 2008). The situation for the other pillar of unpaid domestic work—childcare—is only marginally different: men embrace

© The Author(s) 2018
G. M. Dotti Sani, *Time Use in Domestic Settings Throughout the Life Course*,
SpringerBriefs in Sociology, https://doi.org/10.1007/978-3-319-78720-6_2

childcare more often than housework—it is considered somewhat more enjoyable (Poortman and Van der Lippe 2009)—but women continue to be primarily responsible for the care of their children (Dotti Sani and Treas 2016; Gauthier et al. 2004). Similarly, although kinship ties play a greater role in this respect, women are also more likely to take care of other adults in need, such as an elderly parent (Henz 2010; Lee et al. 2003; Szinovacz and Davey 2008).

However, cross-national research shows that there are important exceptions to this general rule. In some countries domestic work is shared more equally than in others (Dotti Sani 2014; Knudsen and Wærness 2008; Ruppanner et al. 2017) and there are smaller differences in the amount of time women and men spend on housework (Hook 2010) and childcare (Sullivan et al. 2014). For example, studies have shown that in countries that have a long legacy of maternal employment, the division of domestic chores is notably more gender equal (Treas and Tai 2012). In contrast, housework is shared to a lesser extent in countries where men work long standard hours (Dotti Sani 2014). Moreover, empirical studies show that, over time, there has been a shift in the allocation of time given to housework: women are doing less housework than in the past, and their partners are doing slightly more. According to Gershuny: "Women, in each country, and throughout the period, do much more domestic work and much less paid work, than men, and the majority of men's work is certainly paid work … But over time the balances change. The women come to do absolutely more paid and absolutely less unpaid work. The men do generally less paid and increase their unpaid. So the trends for the sexes are clearly convergent" (Gershuny 2000: 6). As for childcare, both mothers and fathers spend more time caring for their children than in the past, and the gender gap has become smaller as men have begun to catch up with women (Bianchi 2000; Dotti Sani and Treas 2016; Gauthier et al. 2004; Maume 2011; Sullivan and Gershuny 2001).

The diminishing of the gender gap in unpaid domestic work goes hand in hand with the increased presence of women in the public sphere: with women's growing educational attainment (Breen et al. 2010) and participation in the labor force (Bettio et al. 2013; Eurostat 2017), men have become more involved in the domestic sphere, both because of women's improved bargaining power within households and because of generalized shifts in behaviour at the societal level (Hook 2010). Nonetheless, researchers speak of an "unfinished revolution" (Gerson 2009), because, despite the significant changes that have taken place over recent decades, women and men are still not sharing equally the burden of domestic work. The inequality is especially evident in some areas of the Western world; Italy is a case in point. If, worldwide, women spend more time on housework and childcare than men, Italian women spend *significantly* more time on domestic chores than their male counterparts. Estimates based on time use data reveal that in the case of an average couple with young children (age 0–5), women spend over 50 hours per week on domestic work (childcare plus housework) while men just above 10 (Anxo et al. 2011). In fact, the authors of this specific study show that the difference is about halved for the same group of subjects in the US and France, and drops to a third in Sweden.

2.1 Gender Inequalities in Domestic Work: An Overview

This unequal division of household labour is of interest to social researchers and policymakers for many reasons. In the Italian context, family welfare is based on a "do it yourself" concept: families provide their own welfare, especially regarding care services. Such responsibility has traditionally been undertaken by Italian women, who embraced the role of full-time homemakers and care givers, while in large part economically sustained by their employed husbands. This situation is referred to as the "male breadwinner" family model (Lewis et al. 2008). However, over preceding decades growing gender-egalitarianism and increasing female educational attainment have brought recent cohorts of young Italian women to compete in the labour market alongside men (Scherer and Reyneri 2008). Moreover, changing labour market regulations, increases in unstable forms of employment and, last but not least, the 2008–2009 economic downturn have strongly increased the need for women to be employed (Karamessini and Rubery 2014); having two salaries has often become a necessary prerequisite for young couples to embrace independent living and to be protected against poverty (Barbieri and Bozzon 2016). Therefore, as Italian women progressively entered the labour market, an increase in men's contribution to the domestic sphere would be a natural expectation. Instead, Italian men still lag behind their European colleagues in the amount of time spent on housework and childcare, leaving Italian women with a "double shift" that is bound to have spill over effects in other areas of life. In particular, the failure to reconcile family and work responsibilities can bring women to refrain from the labour market, reduce their fertility expectations, or—the worst case scenario—both (Del Boca et al. 2004; Dalla Zuanna 2001; Esping-Andersen 2009). Italy has, in fact, unfortunate "lowest low" trends in both fertility and female employment rates (Billari 2004; Dalla Zuanna 2001). It therefore appears that while on the one hand Italian families struggle to have all their members in the labour market, on the other the country lacks a network of services to minimize women's burden of domestic chores and care activities, de facto hindering female employability.

Over recent decades, social scientists from a variety of disciplines, including sociology, psychology and economics, have tried to make sense of the unequal allocation of time to domestic chores between women and men. The main theories accounting for the different amounts of time spent on housework, childcare and adult care by women and men are discussed in the following sections, alongside a discussion of the empirical findings underpinning them.

2.2 The Micro- and Macro-Determinants of Housework

At the individual, micro-level scholars have devised three theoretical perspectives accounting for the individual traits associated with time spent on housework and the division of household tasks between partners. Previous studies and most of the literature cited in this section have focused mainly on working age women and men, generally between 20 and 65 years old, often in couples, often with children. To date, we have accumulated an abundance of research on the micro- and macro-level determinants of time spent on housework in this age range. Research on the time use of older adults is less developed, but it relies largely on the same mechanisms (see Hank and Jürges 2007). In contrast, explanations for time spent on housework by children, teenagers and young adults are slightly different, and are discussed separately in Sect. 2.4.

The *time availability perspective* (Hiller 1984) explains the division of household labour and the allocation of time to housework generally as the result of a rational process, where household tasks are allocated according to the available time of each household member. The main indicators used to measure time constraints are employment status, working hours and schedules, and the presence and number of children in the household. For example, husbands do more domestic chores if their wives are employed outside the home (Davis and Greenstein 2004), and both partners devote more time to domestic chores the more hours they spend at home (Geist 2005). Similarly, in both cross-sectional (Craig et al. 2010) and longitudinal studies (Schober 2013), parenthood is found to increase the domestic work load and also to strengthen a traditional division of labour.

According to the *relative resources perspective*, instead, the allocation of time to domestic work and the division of domestic chores is determined by the level of relative resources (in terms of education and income, for example) each household member brings to the relationship (Blood and Wolfe 1960). For example, research has found that the smaller the wage gap between husband and wife, the more household tasks are equally divided (Blair and Lichter 1991; Greenstein 2000), while men's relatively higher income leads women to do more housework (Geist 2005). Resources have also been operationalized through educational level, and studies have shown that husbands perform more housework when their wives' education is equal to their own or exceeds it (Blair and Lichter 1991; Davis and Greenstein 2004). However, additional education is not linked to financial resources alone, but also to more egalitarian attitudes. Hence, in this case, the higher the husband's educational level, the more likely he is to participate in household tasks (South and Spitze 1994).

The *social construction of gender approach* (Brines 1994; Ferree 1990) argues that the allocation of time given to domestic work and the division of housework is a result of how men and women display their social roles and "produce gender" (Connell 1985; Hochschild 1989; West and Zimmerman 1987, 2009). For example, traditional women are more likely to consider "fair" an unequal division of chores because it matches with the normative standards they embrace (Lavee and Katz 2002).

Beyond the well-established line of research showing that individual characteristics matter for the allocation of time to housework and the division of domestic chores within households, recent studies have found that country characteristics are also relevant in this respect (Treas and Drobnič 2010). It is not surprising that individuals' behaviour is guided by the characteristics of the environment in which they are embedded. Referring to the work by Burt (1987) on structural equivalence, Nazio and Blossfeld put it well: individuals behave not only according to their personal traits, but also according to the "perception of the practice proper for an individual of her position within the social structure" (Nazio and Blossfeld 2003: 52).

The underlying idea behind most studies focusing on the association between macro-level features and micro-level behaviour in housework is that individuals modify their actions based on the changes that take place at the contextual level. In other words, changes in individual behaviour can occur in response to the adoption of the "proper practice," observed at the macro-level, even regardless of personal characteristics (Hook 2006). In relation to housework, there are many structural features that can signal the "proper practice." Hook (2006) provides an example on female employment: "as women's labour force participation affects more men, the bar is set higher when men make social comparisons, creating an across-the-board change in how men "do gender" [...]" (p. 643). Several authors have looked at how female labour force participation and the degree of women's empowerment in societies are related to the division of domestic chores in households (Batalova and Cohen 2002; Fuwa 2004; Knudsen and Wærness 2001). The results have been somewhat inconsistent across studies. Batalova and Cohen (2002), Fuwa (2004) and Ruppanner (2012) on the one hand, show that, in countries where women are more empowered, the division of chores is more equal. Knudsen and Wærness (2008), on the other hand, find no direct effect of women's empowerment on women's share of domestic chores. The results for female labour force participation are also not straightforward. Hook (2006) finds that men perform more housework in countries where women are overall present in the labour market. In a successive study, the author shows that the presence of married women in the workforce increases the time that men spend on cooking and on housework (Hook 2010). Treas and Tai (2012) also show that housework is shared more evenly in countries that have a high legacy of maternal employment, suggesting that female labour force participation has an equalising effect on the division of housework. Fuwa (2004), however, directly tests this hypothesis and finds no effect of female labour force participation on the division of chores within couples. Despite not being fully consistent between studies, these results point toward a relation between women's presence in the public sphere and a more egalitarian division of chores within couples. Other studies have focused on the role of men's aggregate behaviour and have found that when men are more present in the public sphere (e.g. the longer their employment hours) the less they do housework, both in absolute (Hook 2010) and in relative terms (Dotti Sani 2014). Another example is provided by Geist (2005), who applies the welfare regime typology (Esping-Andersen 1990; Korpi 2000) to the division of domestic chores in ten countries and shows that couples are less like to share housework in conservative welfare states regardless of the partners' characteristics, pointing towards the importance of the macro-level context in shaping individual behaviour.

To summarize, research suggests that subjects are influenced by the prevailing norms and behaviours that characterize the surrounding context and act upon them. Thus, even without taking a comparative approach, it is important to keep this in mind when analysing housework in a context of high gender inequality such as Italy. If individuals internalize the gender-traditional norms that are widespread in

Italy, then it is likely that even subjects who could embrace a more gender egalitarian division of domestic labour (such as highly educated couples, women employed full-time and with high earnings) might adopt traditional and thus unequal housework behaviour.

2.3 Theoretical Accounts for Time Spent on Childcare and Adult Care

In much the same way that research shows that women spend more time than men on housework, empirical studies indicate that mothers spend more time than fathers on child-related activities. A gender gap in parental time in childcare emerges in the many countries for which empirical evidence is available (Dotti Sani and Treas 2016; Gauthier et al. 2004; Sayer et al. 2004a). Yet, the gender gap in childcare is smaller than that in housework, perhaps because childcare is perceived as a more rewarding and pleasant activity compared to housework (Poortman and Van der Lippe 2009; Sullivan 2013). As for the determinants of childcare, the literature is centred mostly on the role of time availability, on the one hand, and economic and educational resources on the other. As far as time availability is concerned, unsurprisingly employed parents spend less time on childcare compared to parents who do not work for pay (Craig et al. 2014; Kan et al. 2011). However, among employed mothers, higher earnings predict *more* rather than less time on childcare (Guryan et al. 2008; Kimmel and Connelly 2007), hence "denying the logic of time availability and the opportunity costs of earnings forgone in child care" (Dotti Sani and Treas 2016: 1085). Since higher levels of education are associated with more childcare (England and Srivastava 2013; Sayer et al. 2004b; Sullivan et al. 2014), scholars explain the positive association between earnings and childcare by suggesting that parents with higher earnings are generally also better educated. Highly educated parents place a greater value on the time they spend with their children because they are more aware of the benefits that come from parent-child interaction and are less likely to find suitable substitutes for parental care (Sayer et al. 2004b). Empirical evidence on the positive relationship between maternal higher education and childcare time is unambiguous throughout the Western world (England and Srivastava 2013; Gimenez-Nadal and Molina 2013; Guryan et al. 2008; Lareau 2003; Mancini and Pasqua 2009; Sayer et al. 2004b). In contrast, the association between paternal education and childcare time is subject to more cross-national variation (England and Srivastava 2013; Gimenez-Nadal and Molina 2013; Sullivan et al. 2014).

Alongside individual differences in parental time with children, research has focused on the changes in the societal value placed on childcare (Lareau 2000). Over the past decades both mothers and fathers have been spending more and more time with their children (Bianchi 2000; Dotti Sani and Treas 2016; Gauthier et al. 2004; Maume 2011; Sullivan and Gershuny 2001), suggesting the diffusion of norms that

2.3 Theoretical Accounts for Time Spent on Childcare and Adult Care

encourage involved parenting for both women (Badinter 2012; England and Srivastava 2013; Hays 1996) and men (Duyvendak and Stavenuiter 2004; Henwood and Procter 2003; Hook and Wolfe 2012; Marsiglio et al. 2000; Yoshida 2012).

While parents are those spending more time caring for their children, studies show that grandmothers and grandfathers are also important providers of care. Throughout Europe and beyond, grandparents engage daily in the care of their grandchildren, although the relevance of their involvement varies depending on the national context (Jappens and Bavel 2012). In particular, scholars have noted an association between the availability of public child care and grandparents involvement in childcare (Lewis et al. 2008; Wheelock and Jones 2002). Moreover, research has shown that many of the gender differences that emerge regarding childcare time among parents are also common among grandparents (Craig and Jenkins 2016a, b). In other words, grandmothers are more likely to engage in care activities than grandfathers, and spend more time on them as well. Considering that grandparents are in many cases out of the labour force, explanations based on time availability or relative resources are somewhat less fitting to account for the time they spend caring for their grandchildren, thus suggesting that cultural explanations linked to women's "natural" role as carers might be more likely to explain gender differences in grandchildren care.

Compared to housework and childcare, the allocation of time given to adult care has received somewhat less attention in the sociological literature. The relatively smaller amount of attention paid to this aspect in the scientific debate is rather puzzling, considering the importance of elderly care in ageing societies and the salience of gender inequalities in this respect. Research focused on parental care has shown that women tend to be more involved than men in the care of elderly parents, as they are more likely to be the primary caregivers and to be responsible for the most intensive caregiving tasks (Chesley and Poppie 2009; Henz 2009, 2010; Sarkisian and Gerstel 2004). However, individual level factors beyond gender are highly relevant for time spent caring for parents (Barnett 2013; Henz 2006; Szinovacz and Davey 2008). For example, the importance of kinship in this respect has been highlighted, as studies have found that adult women and men are more likely to take care of their own parents rather than their parents-in-law, albeit with some exceptions (Henz 2010; Lee et al. 2003; Szinovacz and Davey 2008). Economic resources also represent an important source of variation in elder care. Sarkisian and Gerstel (2004) show that controlling for employment status, type of employment and wages explains a large part of the gender gap in time spent caring for elderly parents, while Chesley and Poppie (2009), exploring variations in the type of care provided, show that financial assistance is higher among subjects who work long hours. Finally, factors such as geographical proximity and availability of alternative care givers are also found to play an important role (Szinovacz and Davey 2013). Overall, these studies suggest that teasing out the mechanisms underlying the allocation of time to adult care is more complex compared to housework and childcare and that we need more refined theoretical models and empirical data.

2.4 Explaining Housework Among Children, Adolescents and Young Adults

The theoretical explanations illustrated above and a large part of the empirical studies on housework and childcare in Western countries refer to the allocation of time between adult women and men (Lachance-Grzela and Bouchard 2010) and the division of such chores between partners (Dotti Sani 2014; Fuwa 2004). Only a small body of literature focuses on the time children and teenagers devote to unpaid domestic work. The paucity of studies on children's housework time, especially comparative ones, strongly limits the scholarly understanding of the adoption of early gendered schemes of behaviour. Among the studies that have centred on children's time on unpaid domestic labour, there is a consensus on the finding that girls perform more domestic work than boys, and that the difference is more pronounced when it comes to typically female tasks. In the US, where most of the literature is situated, gender difference in housework for children and adolescents was found in early studies (Blair 1992; Bloch 1987; Gager et al. 1999; Manke et al. 1994). Gager et al. (1999), for example, focus on teenagers using data from the Youth Development Study and find a large gender gap in housework that increases with the teens' age. The result was later confirmed by Gager et al. (2009). Similarly, an early Australian study found that little girls were more likely to engage in what were considered feminine tasks than boys, while boys carried out more masculine tasks than girls (Antill et al. 1996). Focusing on young adults rather than children, Craig et al. (2015) using Australian time use data, find that young women are more likely to engage in indoor routine tasks than young men, while genders do not differ in the probability of engaging in outdoor activities. Results for two Northern European countries are consistent: Evertsson (2006) finds that even in gender equal Sweden, girls spend more time on indoor and family-care work than boys, who are more likely to engage in outdoor tasks compared to girls. Similarly, Bonke (2010), using data for Denmark, shows that boys participate in household chores to a lesser extent than girls. Álvarez and Miles-Touya (2012), for Spain, find that boys spend half the time that girls spend on female-typed housework. For Italy, Belloni and Carriero (2008) employ nationally representative time use data to analyse children's time in various activities and show that girls spend more time on housework than boys. Further, Romano et al. (2012) show that girls tend to perform more female-type tasks (such as food preparation) while boys do male-type tasks (small repairs and outdoor maintenance).

Beyond gender, different theoretical frameworks underpin the relation between children's participation in domestic chores and parental characteristics, such as parents' participation in domestic chores, their education and employment status. From a social constructionist standpoint, children whose parents share housework and engage in gender-atypical tasks are more likely to reproduce a gender equal allocation of tasks (Álvarez and Miles-Touya 2012; Evertsson 2006). Similarly, in terms of the learning of social roles (Bandura 1977), children—and especially boys—are more likely to engage in housework if they see their father take up what is

2.4 Explaining Housework Among Children, Adolescents and Young Adults

considered a typically female task (Cunningham 2001b) rather than if they live in an environment where the mother is the sole person responsible for domestic work. However, fathers who engage in stereotypically female tasks are likely better educated, and as such might not want their offspring to spend time on housework when they could be engaging in other, more productive, activities, for example studying (Bonke 2010). Another parental characteristic that is likely to mediate the relation between parents' and children's housework is maternal employment. Time availability theory, in fact, predicts children's greater involvement in housework when their mother is employed and works full-time (Benin and Edwards 1990; Blair 1992). However, employed mothers are more likely to outsource certain tasks (Van der Lippe et al. 2004; de Ruijter et al. 2005), reducing the burden of domestic work for all household members, including children. Furthermore, maternal employment is strongly associated with maternal attitudes towards the division of labour within households, that in turn affects children's attitudes in this respect (Platt and Polavieja 2016).

A relatively small number of studies, many of which are based on US data, has researched the relation between children's participation in, and time spent on, domestic chores, and the characteristics of the parents. Empirical evidence on the topic is mixed. As for the *direct* link between parents' and children's participation in housework, results from several Western countries suggest that children are more likely to perform gender atypical tasks if their parents do so as well. Cunningham (2001a), for the US, finds that men are more likely to participate in stereotypically female domestic work if their fathers did so when they were children. Similarly, Álvarez and Miles-Touya (2012), using Spanish time use data, show that boys are more likely to engage in female-typed domestic tasks when their father participates in those tasks as well. For Sweden, Evertsson (2006) shows that kids of both genders "are more prone to engage in gender atypical work the more their parent of the same sex engages in this kind of work" (p. 405). By contrast, children do not necessarily do more chores if their parents share them equally (Bonke 2010). Few studies have focused on the "intergenerational transmission" of housework in Italy. In a study on Turin, the second largest city of Northern Italy, Carriero and Todesco (2011) test whether the division of housework of dual earner parents is related to the way their parents shared domestic chores when they were 14 years old. Contrary to the authors' expectations, growing up in a household where parents shared housework equally is not related to the children's division of labour as adults. Romano et al. (2012) employ nationally representative time use data (2002–2003) to investigate whether there is an association between the amount of time mothers and fathers, sons and daughters spend on housework. The authors find that boys are more likely to participate in domestic tasks if the parents share domestic work to some extent.

As for the relation between children's participation in housework and other parental characteristics, the results from empirical studies tend to be mixed and highly contingent on the geographical context and the age of the children. Early studies from the US highlighted a positive association between maternal employment and girls' responsibility for housework (Benin and Edwards 1990; White and

Brinkerhoff 1981). These findings were later confirmed by Blair (1992), per which children substitute employed parents, especially mothers, in housework. Gager et al. (1999), however, do not find a relation between maternal employment and the number of chores that children do. In their later work, Gager et al. (2009) again do not confirm the time-allocation perspective as they show that parental work hours are not associated with children's housework. However, Cunningham (2001a), for the US, finds weak evidence that women perform less stereotypically female housework if their mothers worked during their childhood. Wight et al. (2009) also find no association between teenagers' time in housework and their mother's employment status, while they do show that teenage boys and girls are less likely to do domestic chores if their mothers are high school graduates. As for other Western countries, in a recent study based on Australian time use data, Craig et al. (2015) explore whether the characteristics of co-resident parents and children relate to their allocation of time to different types of routine and non-routine household chores. Their results indicate that parental characteristics, such as educational level and employment hours, are only marginally related to their children's time on housework. Bonke (2010), in Denmark, finds a positive association between maternal full-time employment and children's housework, while parental education reduces the time boys spend on housework, with no effect for girls. For Sweden, Evertsson (2006) finds no relation between the parents' education and their children's housework behaviour, nor with their attitudes towards gender equality at home. Similarly, Cheal (2003) for Canada finds no association between parents' employment status and children's home responsibilities. For Italy, the results by Romano et al. (2012) indicate that maternal employment only marginally increases the amount of time children spend on domestic labour, thus pointing to a small "substitution effect". However, boys are more likely to participate in domestic work if their mother is highly educated and if she is employed. By contrast, daughters of highly educated fathers are less likely to do domestic work. Furthermore, boys (but not girls) take a slightly larger part in cleaning and cooking if their mother is employed than if she is a homemaker. The mother's level of education is relevant to this aspect as well, with children of highly educated mothers more likely to engage in gender atypical tasks.

Considering the ambivalence of parental characteristics for children's time on domestic chores in the contexts described above, the multivariate analyses presented in the following chapters include controls for parental education and employment status.

2.5 Conclusions

To wrap up the theoretical background, previous research has highlighted that many individual and contextual characteristics matter for the allocation of time to domestic work. However, what emerges when contrasting the literature on adults with that for youth is that individual characteristics do not necessarily account for subjects' behaviour throughout the life course and, indeed, some characteristics may well be more relevant during some stages than others. By focusing on individuals in distinct phases of the life course, the following chapters attempt to tease out the relationship between micro-level characteristics and domestic work at different stages of the life cycle.

References

Álvarez, B., & Miles-Touya, D. (2012). Exploring the relationship between parents' and children's housework time in Spain. *Review of Economics of the Household, 10*(2), 299–318.

Antill, J. K., Goodnow, J. J., Russell, G., & Cotton, S. (1996). The influence of parents and family context on children's involvement in household tasks. *Sex Roles, 34*(3–4), 215–236.

Anxo, D., Mencarini, L., Pailhé, A., Solaz, A., et al. (2011). Gender differences in time use over the life course in France, Italy, Sweden, and the US. *Feminist Economics, 17*(3), 159–195.

Badinter, E. (2012). *The conflict: How modern motherhood undermines the status of women*. New York, NY: Metropolitan Books.

Bandura, A. (1977). *Social learning theory*. Oxford, England: Prentice-Hall.

Barbieri, P., & Bozzon, R. (2016). Welfare, labour market deregulation and households' poverty risks: An analysis of the risk of entering poverty at childbirth in different European welfare clusters. *Journal of European Social Policy, 26*(2), 99–123.

Barnett, A. E. (2013). Pathways of adult children providing care to older parents. *Journal of Marriage and Family, 75*(1), 178–190.

Batalova, J. A., & Cohen, P. N. (2002). Premarital cohabitation and housework: Couples in cross-national perspective. *Journal of Marriage and Family, 64*(3), 743–755.

Belloni, C., & Carriero, R. (2008). Il tempo dei bambini [Children's Time]. In Romano (Ed.) *I tempi della vita quotidiana. Un approccio multidisciplinare all'analisi dell'uso del tempo*, pp. 175– 217. Roma: ISTAT.

Benin, M. H., & Edwards, D. A. (1990). Adolescents' chores: The difference between dual-and single-earner families. *Journal of Marriage and the Family*, 361–373.

Bettio, F., Plantenga, J., & Smith, M. (Eds.). (2013). *Gender and the European labour market*. London: Routledge.

Bianchi, S. M. (2000). Maternal employment and time with children: Dramatic change or surprising continuity? *Demography, 37*(4), 401–414.

Billari, F. (2004). Becoming an adult in Europe: A macro (/micro)-demographic perspective. *Demographic Research, 3*, 15–44.

Blair, S. L. (1992). Children's participation in household labor: Child socialization versus the need for household labor. *Journal of Youth and Adolescence, 21*(2), 241–258.

Blair, S. L., & Lichter, D. T. (1991). Measuring the division of household labor: Gender segregation of housework among American couples. *Journal of Family Issues, 12*(1), 91–113.

Bloch, M. N. (1987). The development of sex differences in young children's activities at home: The effect of the social context. *Sex Roles, 16*(5–6), 279–301.

Blood, R., & Wolfe, D. (1960). *Husbands and wives: The dynamics of married living*. New York, NY: Free Press.

Del Boca, D., Pasqua, S., & Pronzato, C. (2004). Why are fertility and women's employment rates so low in Italy? Lessons from France and the U.K. In *IZA Discussion Paper Series* 1274.

Bonke, J. (2010). Children's housework—Are girls more active than boys? *Electronic International Journal of Time Use Research, 7*(1), 1–16.

Breen, R., Luijkx, R., Muller, W., & Pollak, R. (2010). Long-term trends in educational inequality in Europe: Class inequalities and gender differences. *European Sociological Review, 26*(1), 31–48.

Brines, J. (1994). Economic dependency, gender, and the division of labor at home. *American Journal of Sociology*, 652–688.

Burt, R. S. (1987). Social contagion and innovation: Cohesion versus structural equivalence. *American Journal of Sociology, 92*, 1287–1335.

Carriero, R., & Todesco, L. (2011). La divisione del lavoro domestico: l'esempio dei genitori conta? Uno studio a Torino. *Polis, 25*(1), 37–64.

Cheal, D. (2003). Children's home responsibilities: Factors predicting children's household work. *Social Behavior and Personality, 31*(8), 789–794.

Chesley, N., & Poppie, K. (2009). Assisting parents and in-laws: Gender, type of assistance, and couples' employment. *Journal of Marriage and Family, 71*(2), 247–262.

Connell, R. (1985). Theorizing gender. *Sociology, 19*, 260–275.

Craig, L., & Jenkins, B. (2016a). Grandparental childcare in Australia: gender differences in the correlates of providing regular grandparental care while parents work. *Community, Work and Family, 19*(3), 281–301.

Craig, L., & Jenkins, B. (2016b). The composition of parents' and grandparents' child-care time: Gender and generational patterns in activity, multi-tasking and co-presence. *Ageing and Society, 36*(04), 785–810.

Craig, L., Mullan, K., & Blaxland, M. (2010). Parenthood, policy and work-family time in Australia 1992–2006. *Work, Employment and Society, 24*(1), 27–45.

Craig, L., Powell, A., & Brown, J. E. (2015). Co-resident parents and young people aged 15–34: Who does what housework? *Social Indicators Research, 121*(2), 569–588.

Craig, L., Powell, A., & Smyth, C. (2014). Towards intensive parenting? Changes in the composition and determinants of mothers' and fathers' time with children 1992–2006. *The British journal of Sociology, 65*(3), 555–579.

Cunningham, M. (2001a). Parental influences on the gendered division of housework. *American Sociological Review*, 184–203.

Cunningham, M. (2001b). The influence of parental attitudes and behaviors on children's attitudes toward gender and household labor in early adulthood. *Journal of Marriage and Family, 63*(1), 111–122.

Dalla Zuanna, G. (2001). The banquet of Aeolus: A familistic interpretation of Italy's lowest low fertility. *Demographic Research, 4*(5), 133–162.

Davis, S. N., & Greenstein, T. N. (2004). Cross-national variations in the division of household labor. *Journal of Marriage and Family, 66*(5), 1260–1271.

Dotti Sani, G. M. (2012). La divisione del lavoro domestico e delle attività di cura nelle coppie italiane: un'analisi empirica. *Stato e Mercato, 94*(1), 161–192.

Dotti Sani, G. M. (2014). Men's employment hours and time on domestic chores in European countries. *Journal of Family Issues, 35*(8), 1023–1047.

Dotti Sani, G. M., & Treas, J. (2016). Educational gradients in parents' child-care time across countries, 1965–2012. *Journal of Marriage and Family, 78*(4), 1083–1096.

Duyvendak, J. W., & Stavenuiter, M. (2004). Working fathers, caring men. In *Reconciliation of working life and family life*. The Hague, the Netherlands: Ministry of Social Affairs and Employment/Verwey-Jonker Institute.

England, P., & Srivastava, A. (2013). Educational differences in US parents' time spent in child care: The role of culture and cross-spouse influence. *Social Science Research, 42*(4), 971–988.

Esping-Andersen, G. (1990). *The three worlds of welfare capitalism*. Princeton: Princeton University Press.

Esping-Andersen, G. (2009). *The incomplete revolution: Adapting to women's new roles*. Cambridge: Polity.

Eurostat. (2017). *Employment, main characteristics and rates. Annual averages. Code: lfsi_emp_a*. Retrieved July 7, 2017, from http://appsso.eurostat.ec.europa.eu/nui/submitViewTableAction.do.

Evertsson, M. (2006). The reproduction of gender: Housework and attitudes towards gender equality in the home among Swedish boys and girls. *The British Journal of Sociology, 57*(3), 415–436.

References

Ferree, M. M. (1990). Beyond separate spheres: Feminism and family research. *Journal of Marriage and the Family, 50*(4), 866–884.

Fuwa, M. (2004). Macro-level gender inequality and the division of household labor in 22 countries. *American Sociological Review, 69*(6), 751–767.

Gager, C. T., Cooney, T. M., & Call, K. T. (1999). The effects of family characteristics and time use on teenagers' household labor. *Journal of Marriage and the Family*, 982–994.

Gager, C. T., Sanchez, L. A., & Demaris, A. (2009). Whose time is it? The effect of employment and work/family stress on children's housework. *Journal of Family Issues, 30*(11), 1459–1485.

Gauthier, A. H., Smeeding, T. M., & Furstenberg, F. F. (2004). Are parents investing less time in children? Trends in selected industrialized countries. *Population and Development Review, 30*(4), 647–672.

Geist, C. (2005). The welfare state and the home: Regime differences in the domestic division of labour. *European Sociological Review, 21*(1), 23–41.

Geist, C., & Cohen, P. N. (2011). Headed toward equality? Housework change in comparative perspective. *Journal of Marriage and Family, 73*(4), 832–844.

Gershuny, J. (2000). *Changing times: Work and leisure in postindustrial society*. Oxford: Oxford University Press.

Gerson, K. (2009). *The unfinished revolution: How a new generation is reshaping family, work and gender in America*. New York: Oxford University Press.

Gimenez-Nadal, J. I., & Molina, J. A. (2013). Parents' education as a determinant of educational childcare time. *Journal of Population Economics, 26*(2), 719–749.

Greenstein, T. N. (2000). Economic dependence, gender, and the division of labor in the home: A replication and extension. *Journal of Marriage and Family, 62*(2), 322–335.

Guryan, J., Hurst, E., & Kearney, M. (2008). Parental education and parental time with children. *The Journal of Economic Perspectives, 22*(3), 23–46.

Hank, K., & Jürges, H. (2007). Gender and the division of household labor in older couples. *A European perspective, Journal of Family Issues, 28*(3), 399–421.

Hays, S. (1996). *The cultural contradictions of motherhood*. New Haven, CT: Yale University Press.

Henwood, K., & Procter, J. (2003). The "good father": Reading men's accounts of paternal involvement during the transition to first-time fatherhood. *British Journal of Social Psychology, 42*(3), 337–355.

Henz, U. (2006). Informal caregiving at working age: Effects of job characteristics and family configuration. *Journal of Marriage and Family, 68*(2), 411–429.

Henz, U. (2009). Couples' provision of informal care for parents and parents-in-law: Far from sharing equally? *Ageing and Society, 29*(03), 369–395.

Henz, U. (2010). Parent care as unpaid family labor: How do spouses share? *Journal of Marriage and Family, 72*(1), 148–164.

Hiller, D. V. (1984). Power dependence and division of family work. *Sex Roles, 10*(11–12), 1003–1019.

Hochschild, A. (1989). *The second shift: Working parents and the revolution at home*. New York, NY: Viking.

Hook, J. L. (2006). Care in context: Men's unpaid work in 20 countries, 1965–2003. *American Sociological Review, 71*(4), 639–660.

Hook, J. L. (2010). Gender inequality in the welfare state: Sex segregation in housework, 1965–2003. *American Journal of Sociology, 115*(5), 1480–1523.

Hook, J. L., & Wolfe, C. M. (2012). New fathers? Residential fathers' time with children in four countries. *Journal of Family Issues, 33*(4), 415–450.

Jappens, M., & Bavel, J. V. (2012). Regional family cultures and child care by grandparents in Europe. *Demographic Research, 27*(4), 85–120.

Kan, M. Y., Sullivan, O., & Gershuny, J. (2011). Gender convergence in domestic work: Discerning the effects of interactional and institutional barriers from large-scale data. *Sociology, 45*(2), 234–251.

Karamessini, M., & Rubery, J. (2014). *Women and austerity. The economic crisis and the future for gender equality*. New York and Oxon: Routledge.

Kimmel, J., & Connelly, R. (2007). Mothers' time choices: Caregiving, leisure, home production, and paid work. *Journal of Human Resources, 42*(3), 643–681.

Knudsen, K., & Wærness, K. (2001). National context, individual characteristics and attitudes on mothers' employment: A comparative analysis of Great Britain, Sweden and Norway. *Acta Sociologica, 44*(1), 67–79.

Knudsen, K., & Wærness, K. (2008). National context and spouses' housework in 34 countries. *European Sociological Review, 24*(1), 97–113.

Korpi, W. (2000). Faces of inequality: Gender, class, and patterns of inequalities in different types of welfare states. *Social Politics, 7*(2), 127.

Lachance-Grzela, M., & Bouchard, G. (2010). Why do women do the lion's share of housework? A decade of research. *Sex Roles, 63*(11–12), 767–780.

Lareau, A. (2000). Social class and the daily lives of children. A study from the United States. *Childhood., 7*(2), 155–171.

Lareau, A. (2003). *Unequal childhoods: Class, race, and family life*. Berkeley, CA: University of California Press.

Lavee, Y., & Katz, R. (2002). Division of labor, perceived fairness, and marital quality: The effect of gender ideology. *Journal of Marriage and Family, 64*(1), 27–39.

Lee, E., Spitze, G., & Logan, J. R. (2003). Social support to parents-in-law: The interplay of gender and kin hierarchies. *Journal of Marriage and Family, 65*(2), 396–403.

Lewis, J., Campbell, M., & Huerta, C. (2008). Patterns of paid and unpaid work in Western Europe: Gender, commodification, preferences and the implications for policy. *Journal of European Social Policy, 18*(1), 21–37.

Van der Lippe, T., Tijdens, K., & de Ruijter, E. (2004). Outsourcing of domestic tasks and time-saving effects. *Journal of Family Issues, 25*(2), 216–240.

Mancini, A. L., & Pasqua, S. (2009). Asymmetries and interdependencies in time use between Italian spouses. *WP Child, 12*, 2009.

Manke, B., Seery, B. L., Crouter, A. C., & McHale, S. M. (1994). The three corners of domestic labor: Mothers', fathers', and children's weekday and weekend housework. *Journal of Marriage and the Family, 56*(3), 657–668.

Marsiglio, W., Amato, P., Day, R. D., & Lamb, M. E. (2000). Scholarship on fatherhood in the 1990s and beyond. *Journal of Marriage and Family, 62*(4), 1173–1191.

Maume, D. J. (2011). Reconsidering the temporal increase in fathers' time with children. *Journal of Family and Economic Issues, 32*(3), 411–423.

Nazio, T., & Blossfeld, H.-P. (2003). The diffusion of cohabitation among young women in West Germany, East Germany and Italy. *European Journal of Population/Revue Europeenne de Demographie, 19*(1), 47–82.

Platt, L., & Polavieja, J. (2016). Saying and doing gender: Intergenerational transmission of attitudes towards the sexual division of labour. *European Sociological Review, 32*(6), 820–834.

Poortman, A. R., & Van der Lippe, T. (2009). Attitudes toward housework and child care and the gendered division of labor. *Journal of Marriage and Family, 71*(3), 526–541.

Romano, M. C., Mencarini, L., & Tanturri, M. L. (2012). *Uso del tempo e ruoli di genere Tra lavoro e famiglia nel ciclo di vita*. Istituto Nazionale di Statistica.

De Ruijter, E., Treas, J. K., & Cohen, P. N. (2005). Outsourcing the gender factory. *Social Forces, 84*(1), 305–322.

Ruppanner, L. (2012). Housework conflict and divorce: A multi-level analysis. *Work, Employment and Society, 26*(4), 638–656.

Ruppanner, L., Bernhardt, E., & Brandén, M. (2017). Division of housework and his and her view of housework fairness: A typology of Swedish couples. *Demographic Research, 36*, 501–524.

Sarkisian, N., & Gerstel, N. (2004). Explaining the gender gap in help to parents: The importance of employment. *Journal of Marriage and Family, 66*(2), 431–451.

Sayer, L. C., Bianchi, S. M., & Robinson, J. P. (2004a). Are parents investing less in children? Trends in mothers' and fathers' time with children. *American Journal of Sociology, 110*(1), 1–43.

References

Sayer, L. C., Gauthier, A. H., & Furstenberg, F. F. (2004b). Educational differences in parents' time with children: Cross-national variations. *Journal of Marriage and Family, 66*(5), 1152–1169.

Scherer, S., & Reyneri, E. (2008). Come è cresciuta l'occupazione femminile in Italia: fattori strutturali e culturali a confronto. *Stato e Mercato, 83*(2), 183–216.

Schneider, D. (2011). Market earnings and household work: New tests of gender performance theory. *Journal of Marriage and Family, 73*(4), 845–860.

Schober, P. S. (2013). The parenthood effect on gender inequality: Explaining the change in paid and domestic work when British couples become parents. *European Sociological Review, 29*(1), 74–85.

South, S. J., & Spitze, G. (1994). Housework in marital and nonmarital households. *American Sociological Review, 59*(3), 327–347.

Sullivan, O. (2013). What do we learn about gender by analyzing housework separately from child care? Some considerations from time-use evidence. *Journal of Family Theory and Review, 5*(2), 72–84.

Sullivan, O., Billari, F. C., & Altintas, E. (2014). Fathers' changing contributions to child care and domestic work in very low-fertility countries the effect of education. *Journal of Family Issues, 35*(8), 1048–1065.

Sullivan, O., & Gershuny, J. (2001). Cross-national changes in time-use: Some sociological (hi) stories re-examined. *The British Journal of Sociology, 52*(2), 331–347.

Szinovacz, M. E., & Davey, A. (2008). The division of parent care between spouses. *Ageing and Society, 28*(04), 571–597.

Szinovacz, M. E., & Davey, A. (2013). Changes in adult children's participation in parent care. *Ageing and Society, 33*(04), 667–697.

Treas, J., & Drobnič, S. (2010). *Dividing the domestic: Men, women, and household work in cross-national perspective*. Stanford: Stanford University Press.

Treas, J., & Tai, T. (2012). Apron strings of working mothers: Maternal employment and housework in cross-national perspective. *Social Science Research, 41*(4), 833–842.

Treas, J., & Tai, T. (2016). Gender inequality in housework across 20 European nations: Lessons from gender stratification theories. *Sex Roles, 74*(11–12), 495–511.

West, C., & Zimmerman, D. (1987). Doing gender. *Gender and Society, 1*(2), 125–151.

West, C., & Zimmerman, D. (2009). Accounting for doing gender. *Gender and Society, 23*(1), 112–122.

Wheelock, J., & Jones, K. (2002). "Grandparents are the next best thing": Informal childcare for working parents in urban Britain. *Journal of Social Policy, 31*(03), 441–463.

White, L. K., & Brinkerhoff, D. B. (1981). The sexual division of labor: Evidence from childhood. *Social Forces, 60*(1), 170–181.

Wight, V. R., Price, J., Bianchi, S. M., & Hunt, B. R. (2009). The time use of teenagers. *Social Science Research, 38*(4), 792–809.

Yoshida, A. (2012). Dads who do diapers: Factors affecting care of young children by fathers. *Journal of Family Issues, 33*(4), 451–477.

Chapter 3
The Italian Time Use Survey

Abstract This chapter provides an overview of how time use can be studied and what empirical strategies are adopted in this volume to study time in the domestic sphere. Specifically, the chapter illustrates the Italian Time Use Survey and its main strengths, in particular the diary method technique for data collection and its large sample size. The chapter then describes the life course approach adopted in the volume and the main dependent variables used in the empirical chapters: overall housework and its main sub-components (cooking, washing clothes and cleaning the house, odd jobs), childcare and its sub-components (physical childcare, interactive childcare, helping with homework), and adult care. Then the main independent variables are discussed. Finally, the chapter provides a graphic and descriptive overview of the time spent by women and men on general housework, childcare and adult care across all the stages of the life course considered in the volume.

Keywords Domestic work · Housework · Childcare · Adult care
Life course · Italy · Italian time use survey

3.1 Time Use Data: What Is It and How Can We Use It?

The literature discussed in the previous chapter provides hefty evidence about the unequal allocation of housework, childcare and adult care in cross-national perspective and the peculiar Italian case. The scope of the following chapters is to further deepen our knowledge of domestic work in Italy by offering a detailed account of domestic time and participation at different stages of the life course, from childhood (Chap. 4) to older age (Chap. 8). Before delving, chapter by chapter, into the age-specific results, this chapter provides an overview of how time use can be studied and what empirical strategies are adopted in the volume to study time use in the domestic sphere.

© The Author(s) 2018
G. M. Dotti Sani, *Time Use in Domestic Settings Throughout the Life Course*,
SpringerBriefs in Sociology, https://doi.org/10.1007/978-3-319-78720-6_3

3.2 The Italian Time Use Survey

The analyses presented in this volume are based on data from the Italian Time Use Survey (TUS) collected by the Italian National Institute of Statistics (ISTAT 1988–1989, 2002–2003, 2008–2009, 2013–2014). The Italian TUS collects data through a daily time use diary where individuals are asked to report their activities for a 24 h period, starting at 4 am. Time diaries are known to provide more accurate time use data compared to other ways of collecting information on how individuals spend their time, such as questionnaire items asking how much time respondents usually spend on certain activities (Schulz and Grunow 2012). Time diaries are especially recommended to avoid recall bias in particular categories of subjects, such as children (Ben-Arieh and Ofir 2002). The Italian TUS also includes a week-long diary focused exclusively on time devoted to paid work and a questionnaire colleting respondents' background information. Compared to other national time use surveys, the Italian TUS has the important feature of sampling entire households, so that all members—adults, elderly and children[1]—fill in their daily time use diary. This valuable characteristic allows us to study not just individual time use but also collective "family" time. Since background information on all household members is available, it is also possible to investigate how subjects' time use is associated with the characteristics of other family members. For example, the data allow estimating whether there is an association between children's time on domestic chores and their parents' time on housework, level of education and employment status. Similarly, we can estimate the share of housework performed by partnered women and men while controlling for both partners' characteristics.

Secondary data are rarely perfect, and the Italian TUS is no exception. One of the limitations of the data lies in its cross-sectional nature, which impedes following subjects over time to evaluate how their behaviour changes over the life course. The strategy adopted in the volume to overcome this limitation is to provide an accurate and comprehensive description of domestic time among individuals at different stages of the life cycle. A second limitation, which is quite common to time use data, lies in having to rely on information for only one day—the diary day— regardless of whether this was a routine or out of the ordinary day. Furthermore, as will be discussed in later chapters, diary data provided for a single day lessen the probability of capturing unlikely and/or occasional activities.

As of today, the Italian National Institute of Statistics has collected four waves of time use data, specifically in 1988–89, 2002–03, 2008–09 and 2013–14. Each wave comprises approximatively 20,000 households for a total of about 40,000 individuals. For the analyses of the book we rely on the most recent wave. However, we shall also exploit the repeated-wave design to describe how time in housework and childcare has changed from 1988–89 to 2013–14. The respondents in the sampled households were asked to keep their diary on a specific day of the week, to ensure

---

[1]Children in the Italian TUS fill in their own diary unless they are unable to do so, in which case the main caregiver is asked to provide the information.

3.2 The Italian Time Use Survey

that data are available for both weekdays and weekends. This detail is important for the study of housework, an activity that is not homogenously spread over the week (Manke et al. 1994; Neilson and Stanfors 2014). Indeed, the temporal rhythms of Italian households see children in school and employed parents at work from Monday to Friday for relatively long hours. Therefore, institutionalized time might impose greater time binds on weekdays than on weekends. Hence, not only participation in domestic work might vary by day of the week, but family characteristics might also play different roles depending on the available amount of free time on the diary day. For this reason, we control for day of the week in the multivariate analyses.

To get an idea of the type of detail that the Italian TUS allows us to reach, Fig. 3.1 shows the time use patterns on an average day for Italian women (left side) and men (right side) aged 20–64. The area-plots presented in the figure are obtained by calculating the percentages of women and men who engaged in eight main activities during the diary day: sleep and personal care, meals, paid work, housework, childcare, adult care, leisure and travel. The percentages of subjects engaged in each activity are then plotted against the time of day during which the activities took place. This simple exercise allows us to observe some crucial distinctions in the time use patterns of working age women and men. Beyond important regularities in time use—such as sleeping patterns and the two peaks for meals around 1.30 and 20.30 pm—the figure shows that there are three large differences in the

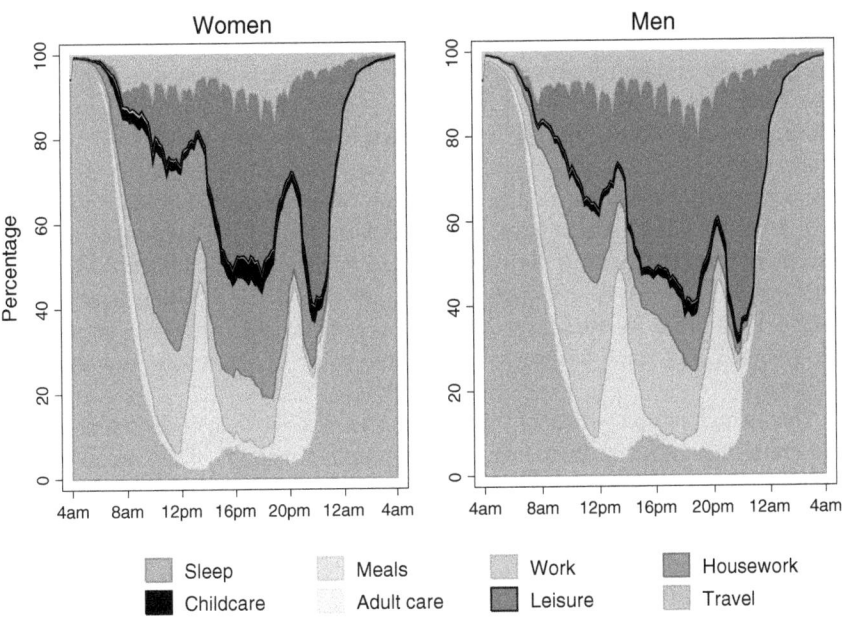

Fig. 3.1 Average daily time-use patterns for women and men aged 20–64. ISTAT TUS 2013–14. Unweighted values. Own calculations

way Italian women and men spend their day. First, men are much more likely to be doing paid work than women; second, women are much more likely to be doing housework, and to a smaller extent childcare and adult care than men; third, men are more likely to be enjoying leisure activities compared to women. These average differences leave ample room for detailed analyses of time use among individuals with different characteristics—both within and between genders—which are discussed in the following sections and chapters.

3.3 Gauging the Life Cycle: Respondents Age-Groups

To investigate domestic work over the life course, respondents are divided into groups according to their age and their position in the life cycle. Specifically, the sample is subset following an ideal typical line going from childhood to maturity passing through crucial stages such as leaving the parental home, living with a partner, becoming a parent, and the empty nest phase. Within each of these main stages, respondents are clustered based on their age. This two-step process leads to the formation of the following groups,[2] graphically summarized in Fig. 3.2.

The first group consists of sons and daughters living in two-parent households (Chap. 4). We limit the analyses to two parent-dwellings as these represent the vast majority of Italian households (OECD 2017). Single parent families require a separate study because they might have a less traditional approach toward gender role socialization (Leve and Fagot 1997). Since children's age is relevant for their participation in chores (Álvarez and Miles-Touya 2012; Dotti Sani 2016) within this group we distinguish between seven age clusters likely characterized by similar time binds: pre-school children (aged 3–5), primary school children (aged 6–10), middle school children (aged 11–14), high school children (aged 15–19), young adults (aged 20–24), adults (aged 25–34) and older adults (over 35 years old). Issues of sample selection might arise among older children (e.g. above 20 years old), as some young adults might have permanently left the household or reside elsewhere for large parts of the year (for example university students). The very high age at home leaving in Italy (Billari 2004) and the fact that over 50% of Italians aged 20 to 34 lives with their parents (OECD 2017) limits to some extent the selection, but some caution in the interpretation of the results is nonetheless required.

The second group consists of subjects who have moved out of the parental home and are living either on their own or in a couple (Chap. 5). The crucial element defining this group is being childless. These subjects have made the first step in the transition to adulthood defined by leaving the parental home but do not yet have

---

[2]As mentioned, the focus of the volume lies within these relatively broad groups that correspond to common stages of a "typical" life course. Due to limited number of cases, we cannot spend many words on relatively small groups and the analyses are restricted to these main life course stages.

3.3 Gauging the Life Cycle: Respondents Age-Groups

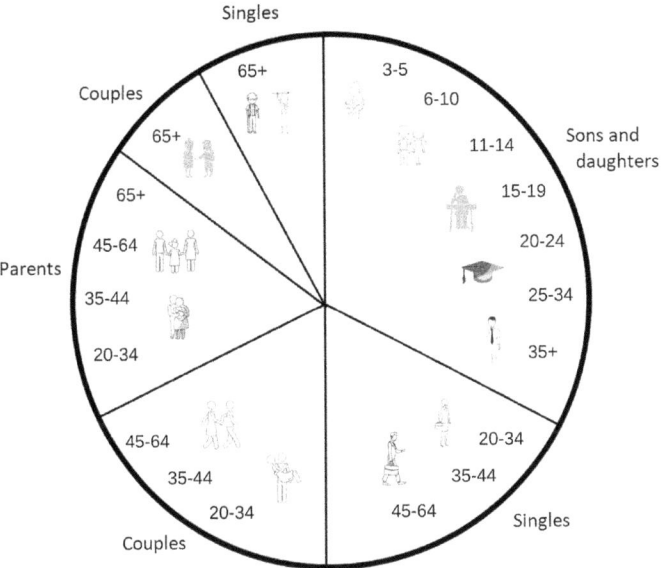

Fig. 3.2 Graphic overview of life course stages

children. Within this stage we distinguish four clusters: childless singles aged 20–34 and 35–44 and childless couples aged 20–34 and 35–44.

Parenthood defines the third group, which is further subset into clusters based on the age of the parents and the age of the children. For the descriptive purpose of the current chapter we distinguish between parents aged 20–34 years, 35–44 and 45–64. However, in Chaps. 6 and 7 we use a more fine-tuned distinction between parents of younger children (i.e. aged 14 and below) and parents of older children (i.e. aged 15 and above). Chapter 7 includes also childless adults aged 45–64 to allow an additional comparison.

Finally, in Chap. 8 we look at older adults, that is respondents aged 65 and above. In this age-group we distinguish between parents with children living in the household, parents whose children have moved out, singles whose children have moved out, childless couples, and childless singles.

3.4 Analysing Housework, Childcare and Adult Care

3.4.1 Measures

Several types of domestic work are analysed throughout the volume. The following sections detail what activities are considered within the broader categories of housework, childcare and adult care.

Housework. The main housework variable used throughout the volume comprises a wide array of domestic work activities such as cooking, setting the table, washing dishes and cleaning the kitchen; taking out the garbage, cleaning and tidying up the house and outdoor areas; doing the laundry and ironing; gardening and taking care of pets; repairing and decorating the house, taking care of the car and other vehicles; shopping and purchasing goods and services and various household management tasks. Research has shown, however, that housework is not a homogenous task, and that some activities can be considered typically female, others typically male and some gender-neutral. To tap into this aspect, three additional variables measure gender-typical activities: cooking and all related activities such as setting the table and washing the dishes (typically female); washing clothes and cleaning the house (typically female); all the remaining odd types of housework, including shopping, vehicle maintenance, gardening and do it yourself activities (typically male or gender-neutral activities).

Childcare. Four childcare variables are used in the volume. For preliminary descriptive purposes, we rely on a variable including all childcare activities. For more detailed analyses, we distinguish between physical childcare and interactive childcare. Physical childcare refers to all the activities that concern children's physical well-being such as changing diapers, feeding infants, giving baths and dressing children. The variable also includes less time-intensive activities such as child supervision and taking children to and from child-related activities (e.g. going and coming from school, the playground, a playdate, etc.). In contrast, interactive childcare refers to activities that involve a structured parent-child interaction. We distinguish between (i) helping the children do their homework and (ii) reading, talking, and playing with infants and children. It is instructive to distinguish between the two types of activities because based on their age children have a greater need for one or the other. Moreover, certain parental characteristics, in particular education, are known to favour interactional over physical childcare (see Hsin 2009).

Adult care. The adult care category includes general physical care and medical assistance towards ill or disabled adult family members, as well as providing company and taking adults in need to places, for example to a doctor's appointment. Indirect care, such as helping adult family members in various activities is also part of this category.

3.4.2 Analyses

Four different types of dependent variables are used to analyse the various components of domestic work. First, absolute minutes per day are used to calculate and report average time on each of the activities of interest. These averages are calculated on the entire sample and therefore include those respondents who spent 0 min on domestic work on the diary day. Second, we focus on the percentage of respondents who took part in each of the considered forms of domestic work (the doers). Third, we consider the absolute minutes per day spent on domestic work by the subsample of doers. Fourth, when focusing on couples we use a relative measure of time spent on the different components of domestic work by each partner. The four measures combined allow us to depict a fine-grained picture of domestic work across different stages of the life course.

The variables are qualitatively different, therefore specific data analysis techniques are used. Standard OLS regression[3] is used to model the minutes per day spent on the various types of domestic work (overall and on the subsample of doers). Logistic regression models are used to estimate the probability of engaging in domestic chores; and, finally, a generalized linear model with the logit link and the binomial family is used to estimate the relative time on domestic work spent by partners. Throughout the book, predicted values and predicted probabilities are used to illustrate the results alongside the model coefficients (Long and Freese 2014).

3.4.3 Independent Variables

Gender is the most relevant variable when studying housework. Therefore, descriptive results and multivariate analyses are always presented separately by gender. The multivariate models also control for potentially confounding variables used in previous studies (Cunningham 2001; Dotti Sani 2014; Henz 2006; Lachance-Grzela and Bouchard 2010). When modeling housework, childcare and adult care among adults, we always control for their level of education (low education, i.e. less than secondary education, as reference category versus medium education, i.e. completed secondary, and high, i.e. above secondary education) and employment status (employed as omitted reference category vs. not being employed, that is, homemakers, unemployed, retired and others). We also control for age group, marital status (married vs. cohabiting), number and age of the children in the household, day of the week (weekend vs. weekday) and area of residence using five macro areas (North West as reference category, North East, Centre, South, Islands[4]). When analysing couples, we also add a measure indicating who is the main breadwinner in the household (partners earn about the same amount as reference category vs. the respondent earns more than partner, the respondent earns less than the partner). The models for children include all the above, plus the parents' level of education and employment status, as well as

---

[3]Tobit models are sometimes recommended to account for the skewed distribution of time use variables. However, studies have shown only limited differences between the estimates produced by Tobit and standard OLS models (Stewart 2013). Therefore, we opted for the more common Ordinary Least Square models.

[4]North East: Trentino Alto-Adige, Veneto, Friuli-Venezia Giulia, Emilia Romagna. North West: Piemonte—Valle d'Aosta, Lombardia, Liguria. Centre: Toscana, Umbria, Marche, Lazio. South: Abruzzo, Molise, Campania, Basilicata, Calabria, Puglia. Islands: Sicilia and Sardegna.

paternal time and participation in domestic work. Summary statistics for the relevant independent variables are reported in each of the empirical chapters.

3.5 Housework, Childcare and Adult Care Over the Life Course

The following sections illustrate time on and participation in housework, childcare and adult care—the three pillars of unpaid domestic work—among women and men in different stages of the life course.

3.5.1 Housework

We begin our analysis by graphically displaying housework time and participation among women and men of different ages and stages of life (Figs. 3.3, 3.4, 3.5 and 3.6). Each figure is composed of three panels that report, respectively, the average minutes spent on general housework, participation in housework, and average minutes spent on housework by respondents who engaged in this activity for at least 10 min on the diary day. The values for all age groups are summarized in Table 3.1.

Starting from children living in the parental home, panel (a) in Fig. 3.3 shows that girls spend more time on general housework than boys at all ages except among children aged 3–5. Notably, the gender gap becomes wider among older children: girls do 16 min more housework than boys among children aged 11–14, and at age 15–19 the gap is over half an hour (26 min for boys and 58 min for girls). The gender gap continues to increase as children grow and peaks among adults over 35 years old living in the parental home. Here, men do about 76 min of housework per day and women about 204 min (3 h and a half). Looking at differences in participation rather than absolute time, panel (b) shows that gender differences among pre-school children are small. Participation in this group is surprisingly high (nearly 30%), likely because children younger than 5 years old spend more time at home compared to kids in primary school, and parents have more chances to involve them in simple domestic chores like watering plants and feeding pets. In contrast, the gender gap in participation becomes evident among children aged 6–10, grows progressively wider among older children and peaks among sons and daughters aged 25–34 (nearly 40 percentage points difference). A large gender gap persists among women and men aged 35 and older, with about 60% of men engaging in general housework on an average day compared to nearly 90% of women. Finally, panel (c) shows that gender differences in housework time emerge even among children who engaged in this activity, although the gender gap only becomes evident starting from children aged 11–14. These descriptive results

3.5 Housework, Childcare and Adult Care Over the Life Course

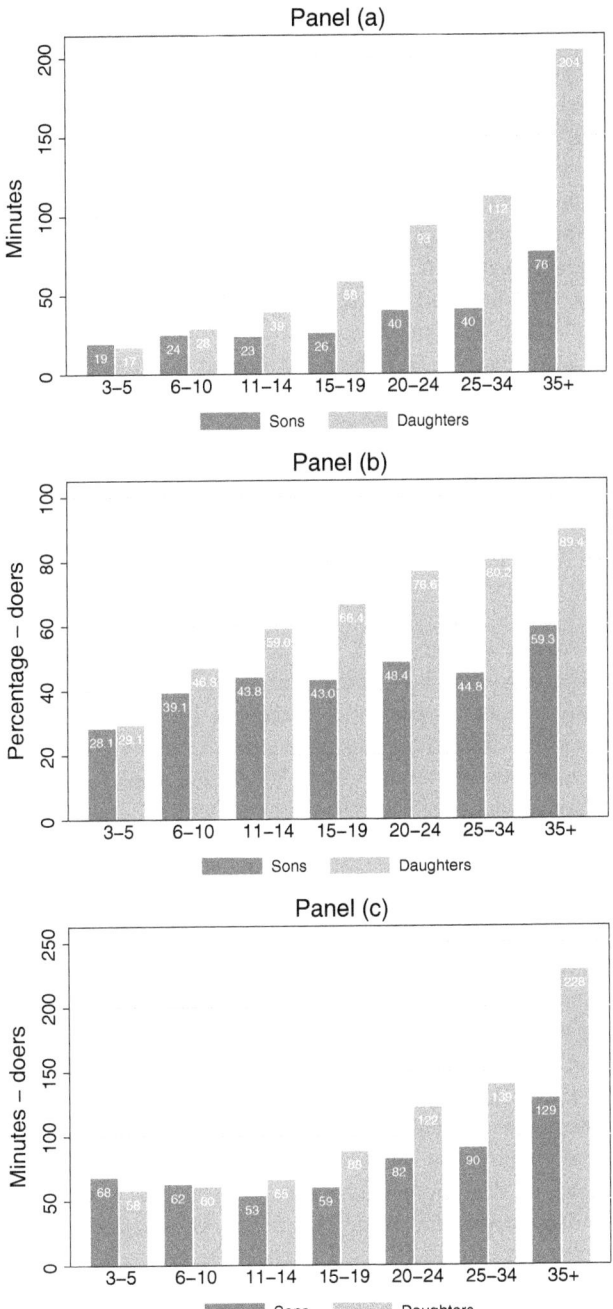

Fig. 3.3 Housework among daughters and sons living in the parental home. Panel (**a**): average minutes of housework on the diary day. Panel (**b**): percentage of subjects engaged in housework on the diary day. Panel (**c**): average minutes of housework among subjects who engaged in at least ten minutes of housework on the diary day. ISTAT TUS 2013–14. Unweighted values. Own calculations

suggest that gender inequalities in domestic work are deeply rooted in childhood and are likely to continue in adulthood.

We now focus on housework among childless young women and men who have left the parental home and are living either on their own or in couples and are between 20 and 34, or 35 and 44 years old. Panel (a) in Fig. 3.4 shows that women do more housework than men in all four groups, and that they increase the amount of housework they do as they progress through life from being single to being in a relationship. Single women aged 20–34 do about 2 h and 20 min of housework per day, while single women aged 35–44 spend 2 h and 40 min. Coupled women spend even more time on housework: about 3 h and a half in both age groups (209 and 219 min respectively). Time on housework among men shows much less variation, as men in all four groups spend about 90 min on housework daily. Panel (b) in Fig. 3.4 shows that there are little within-gender differences in participation rates across the four groups. About 90% of women in all four groups did some housework on the diary day, with a peak of 98% among the older group of coupled women. The values for men are close to 75% across groups. Panel (c) shows the patterns of time use for the doers, that is for those who did at least 10 min of housework on the diary day. The within- and between-gender differences are similar to those in panel (a), despite the values being somewhat higher for obvious reasons.

Gender differences in housework time and participation peak among parents. The panels in Fig. 3.5 report housework time, participation, and time for those who participated among coupled parents in three age groups: 20–34, 35–44, 45–64. Panel (a) shows that mothers spend an enormous amount of time on domestic chores compared to fathers. Mothers aged 20–34 and aged 35–44 spend about 4 h and a half on housework, while fathers about 1 h and a half. Among parents aged 45–64, mothers spend 5 h and a half doing domestic work and fathers 1 h and 50 min. Differences in housework participation are also striking: while nearly 100% of mothers engaged in housework on the diary day, the values for fathers in the three groups are, respectively, 72, 74 and 76%. Given their very high participation rate, the values for mothers' absolute time among the doers in panel (c) are basically identical of those from panel (a). For fathers, in contrast, there is a substantial increase, suggesting that when fathers participate, they do so for reasonably large amounts of time, albeit being very far from matching mothers' time on housework. The large gender differences that emerge suggest that parenthood leads to task specialization between women and men in unpaid work and probably also in other domains, such as employment. These aspects will be discussed more in depth in the chapters focusing on the micro- and meso- determinants of parents' housework, childcare and adult care (Chaps. 6 and 7). Housework time and participation among

3.5 Housework, Childcare and Adult Care Over the Life Course

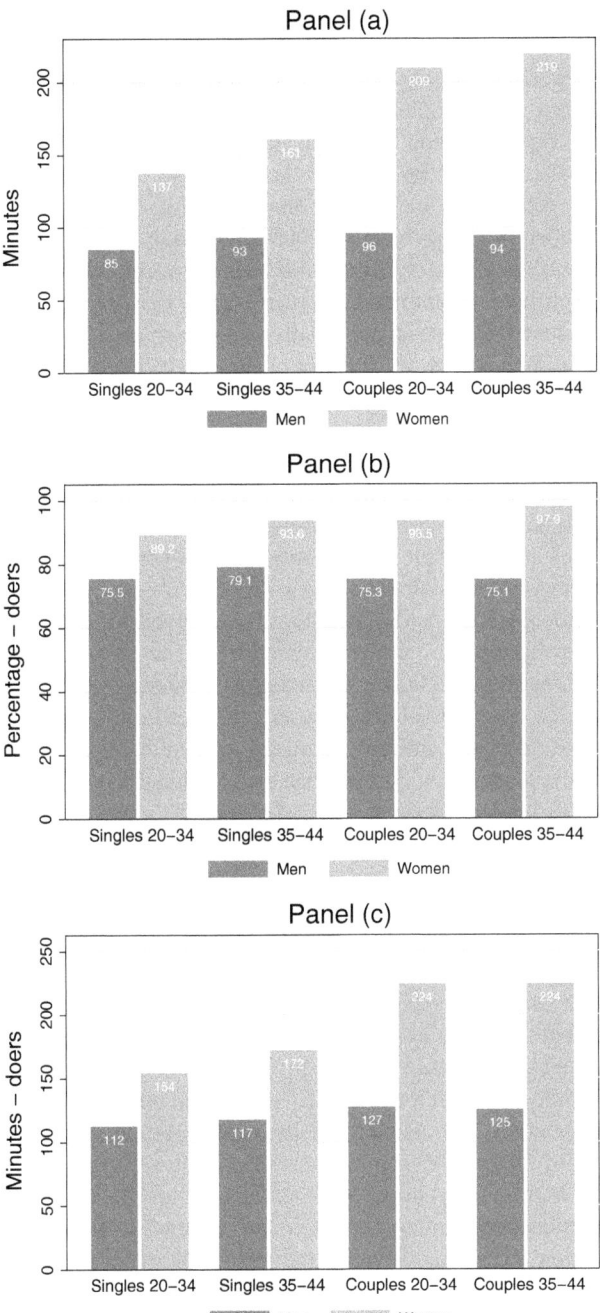

Fig. 3.4 Housework among childless women and men, aged 20–44. Panel (**a**): average minutes of housework on the diary day. Panel (**b**): percentage of subjects engaged in housework on the diary day. Panel (**c**): average minutes of housework among subjects who engaged in at least ten minutes of housework on the diary day. ISTAT TUS 2013–14. Unweighted values. Own calculations

single parents are not reported but the results are substantially in line with those for coupled parents. However, single fathers spend more time on housework compared to partnered fathers, while single mothers do less than their coupled counterparts. This suggests that gender differences in housework time are somewhat reduced in absence of task specialization, although the time constraints for single working mothers could also account for some of this variation.

Finally, Fig. 3.6 reports housework among adults aged 65 and above. These subjects are divided in groups based on their partnership status (singles vs. couples) and parental status (never had children, children have moved out of the parental home, children living at home). Starting from panel (a), it is worthy to note that gender differences in housework time are the smallest among singles. Indeed, single men do about 170 min of housework per day. The values for coupled men are considerably lower: 122, 135 and 148 min per day among men in childless couples, fathers whose children have left the parental home, and fathers living with a partner and children respectively. The differences between single and partnered men suggest that men invest more time in domestic work when they cannot offload it to a female partner. Not surprisingly, women do much more housework than men in all age groups, but the values are lower among single women, especially when children are not present. Partnered mothers with children at home do the largest amount of housework (364) while partnered mothers whose children have moved out and partnered childless women do somewhat less (327 and 322 respectively). These results suggest, therefore, that women's domestic workload is considerably lighter if they do not have to take care of anyone else. Another distinctive pattern emerges from the participation rates of panel (b) that are close to or above 90% among women in all groups, and about 80% among men in all groups. Thus, both women and men have very high chances of doing at least 10 min of housework on the diary day. Finally, panel (c) shows the average daily minutes of housework among the doers. The results confirm that the gender gap in domestic chores is smallest among single women and men, thus underlining again the relevance of task specialization in accounting for women's very high time on housework.

There are several considerations that can be drawn from these data. First, gender differences in absolute time spent on general housework are evident at every stage of the life course with the only exception of very young children. Second, women are more likely to engage in housework on a given day compared to men, again with the exception of children aged 3–5. Hence, women do more housework than men throughout their entire life course, due to greater participation and greater time investment. Third, the gender gap in housework time and participation is smallest among singles, both in the younger and older age groups. Indeed, single women do less housework than their partnered counterparts, and men do more. This suggests that task specialization is a strong driver of the large bulk of housework performed by Italian women.

3.5 Housework, Childcare and Adult Care Over the Life Course

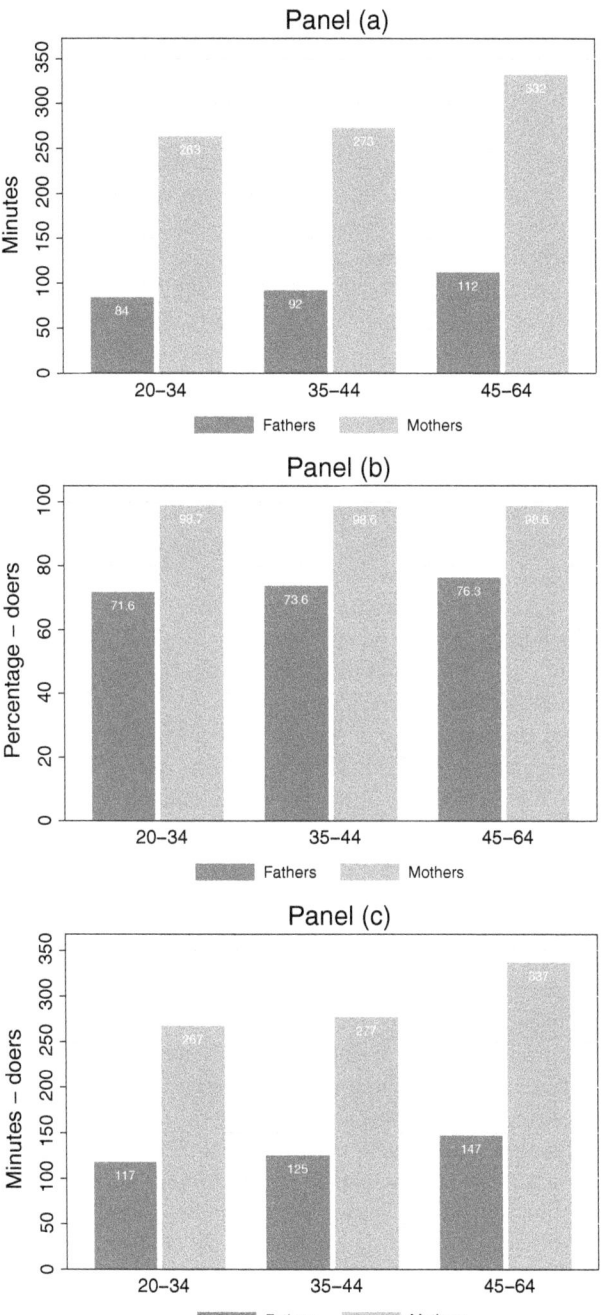

Fig. 3.5 Housework among parents aged 20–64. Panel (**a**): average minutes of housework on the diary day. Panel (**b**): percentage of subjects engaged in housework on the diary day. Panel (**c**): average minutes of housework among subjects who engaged in at least ten minutes of housework on the diary day. ISTAT TUS 2013–14. Unweighted values. Own calculations

3.5.2 Childcare

This section focuses on parents and considers gender differences in childcare time and participation. A preliminary consideration to make is that childcare time varies not only by age of the parents, but also by age of the children. Younger children require extensive physical and interactive care while older children are more autonomous in both respects. At the same time, parents' and children's ages tend to be highly correlated. Indeed, from a cross-sectional perspective we observe that younger parents tend to have younger children while older parents, on average, have older children. Thus, in Chaps. 6 and 7 we focus on parents of younger and older children, respectively, to keep into consideration both the age of the parents and the age of the children. For the current descriptive analyses, instead, we subset the sample of parents into three age groups: from 20 to 34, from 35 to 44 and from 45 to 64.

For the three groups, Fig. 3.7 shows the average minutes spent on childcare in panel (a); the percentages of parents involved in childcare on the diary day in panel (b); and the average minutes spent on childcare among parents who did at least ten minutes of childcare on the diary day in panel (c). Younger parents spend considerably more time on childcare compared to older ones. However, gender differences are much larger among parents aged 20–34 than among older ones. In the youngest age group, mothers spend about 2 h and 20 min in childcare related activities, while fathers one hour and 19 min. In the 35–44 age group fathers do about one hour of childcare and mothers one hour and a half. The gender difference disappears among parents between 45 and 64 years old. Similar patterns emerge when looking at the percentages of parents doing childcare: mothers engage more than fathers (91% vs. 74% in the 20–34 age group), but differences are smaller among older parents. Among parents who did at least 10 min of childcare on the diary day, mothers outperform fathers in the two younger age groups, while fathers do more childcare in the older group. The differences that emerge from these figures are largely accounted for by younger parents having younger children who require much more childcare.

This aspect is explored in the panels in Fig. 3.8, that show the daily minutes parents spend on all childcare in panel (a), physical childcare in panel (b), and interactive childcare—distinguishing between playing and verbally interacting with children in panel (c) versus helping with homework in panel (d)—conditioning on the age of the youngest child. Panel (a) shows that children's need for general care decreases as they grow: mothers whose youngest child is below age 2 spend over three hours of childcare on the diary day and fathers nearly 1 h and 40 min. The values quickly drop and, by the time the youngest child is age 9, mothers spend about 1 h per day and fathers about 30 min on overall care. The gender gap is narrowed down among parents of older children and general childcare time progressively approaches zero by the time the youngest child is in middle school (aged 11–14). Panel (b) shows a similar result for physical childcare: mothers spend more time on this set of activities than fathers when children are very young and the

3.5 Housework, Childcare and Adult Care Over the Life Course

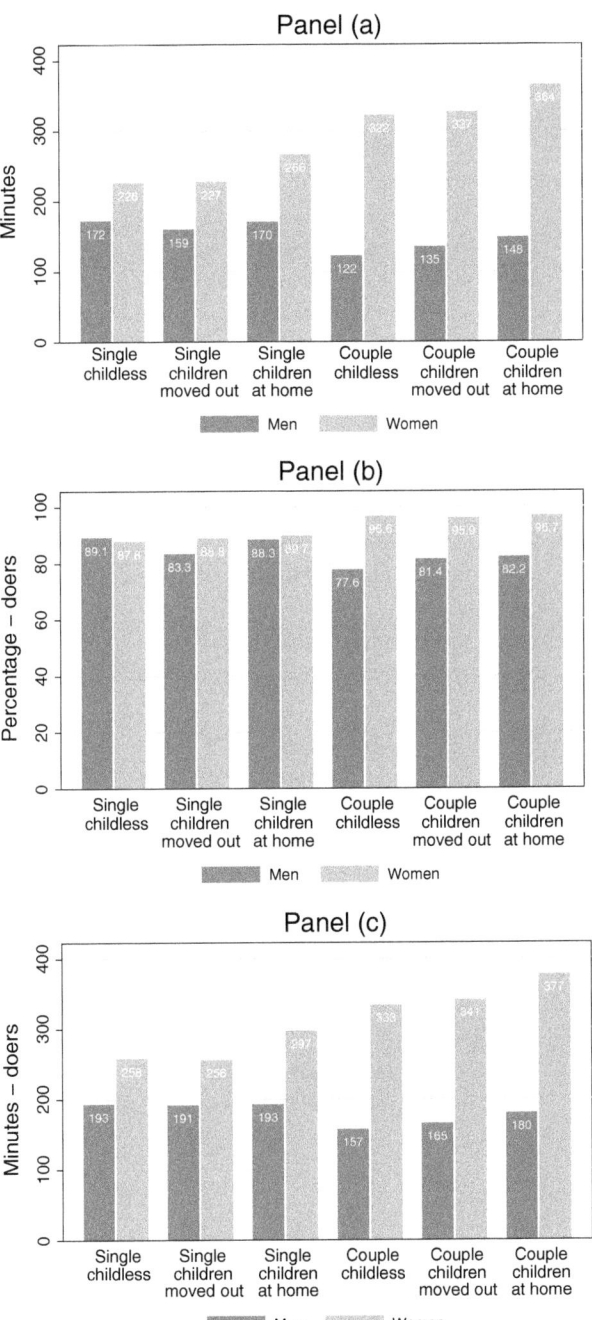

Fig. 3.6 Housework among adults aged 65 and above. Panel (**a**): average minutes of housework on the diary day. Panel (**b**): percentage of subjects engaged in housework on the diary day. Panel (**c**): average minutes of housework among subjects who engaged in at least ten minutes of housework on the diary day. ISTAT TUS 2013–14. Unweighted values. Own calculations

Table 3.1 General housework time and participation. ISTAT TUS 2013–2014. Unweighted values. Own calculations

	Men					Women				
	All subjects			Doers		All subjects			Doers	
	Min	%	N	Min	N	Min	%	N	Min	N
Living in the parental home										
3–5	19	28	519	68	146	17	29	478	58	139
6–10	24	39	917	62	359	28	47	899	60	421
11–14	23	44	812	53	356	39	59	770	65	454
15–19	26	43	986	59	424	58	66	972	88	645
20–24	40	48	878	82	425	93	77	918	122	703
25–34	40	45	1098	90	492	112	80	873	139	700
≥35	76	59	805	129	477	204	89	584	228	522
Single, childless										
20–34	85	75	363	112	274	137	89	249	154	222
35–44	93	79	421	117	333	161	94	297	172	278
45–64	130	82	553	159	452	204	96	532	213	511
≥65	172	89	303	193	270	226	88	564	258	495
Single, children left parental home										
45–64	126	83	369	151	308	232	96	450	240	434
≥65	159	83	473	191	394	227	89	1829	256	1625
Couple, childless										
20–34	96	75	194	127	146	209	94	279	224	261
35–44	94	75	261	125	196	219	98	234	224	229
45–64	120	79	410	152	325	274	97	441	281	429
≥65	122	78	313	157	243	322	97	238	333	230
Couple, children left parental home										
45–64	133	79	657	167	521	319	98	1022	326	1001
≥65	135	81	2096	165	1707	327	96	1692	341	1623
Parents										
20–34	84	72	398	117	285	263	99	768	267	758
35–44	92	74	1556	125	1145	273	99	1884	277	1857
45–64	112	76	3478	147	2653	332	99	3112	337	3069
≥65	148	82	741	180	609	364	97	426	377	412

3.5 Housework, Childcare and Adult Care Over the Life Course

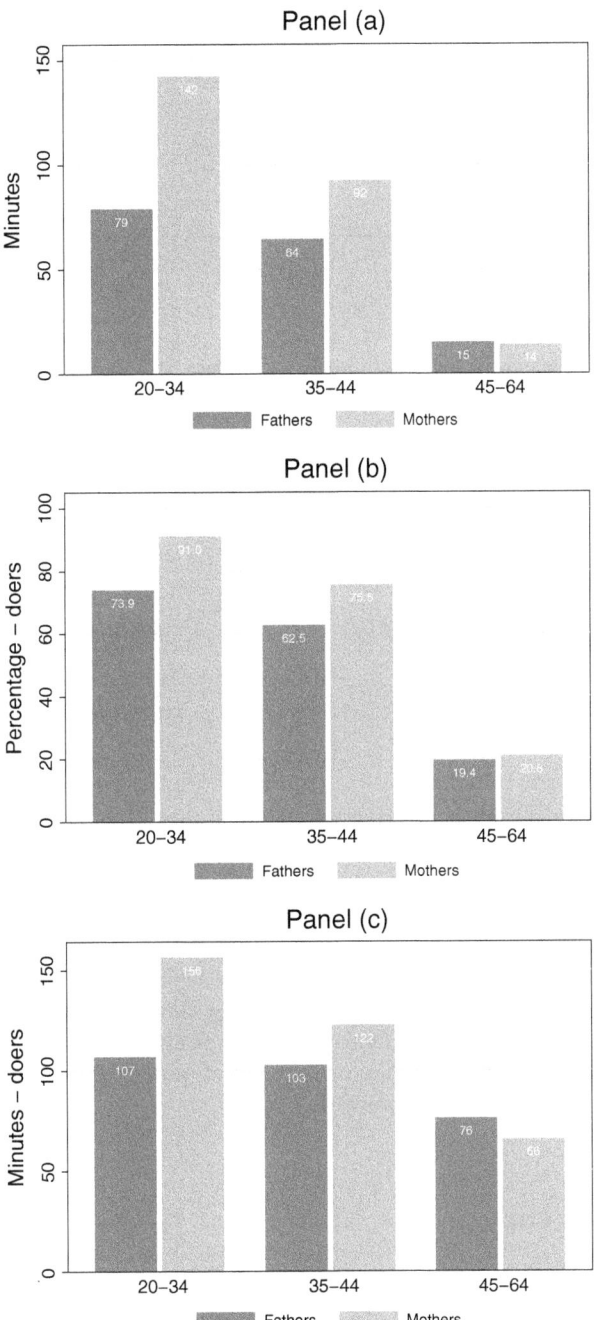

Fig. 3.7 Childcare among mothers and fathers aged 20–64. Panel (**a**): average minutes of housework on the diary day. Panel (**b**): percentage of subjects engaged in housework on the diary day. Panel (**c**): average minutes of housework among subjects who engaged in at least 10 min of housework on the diary day. ISTAT TUS 2013–14. Unweighted values. Own calculations

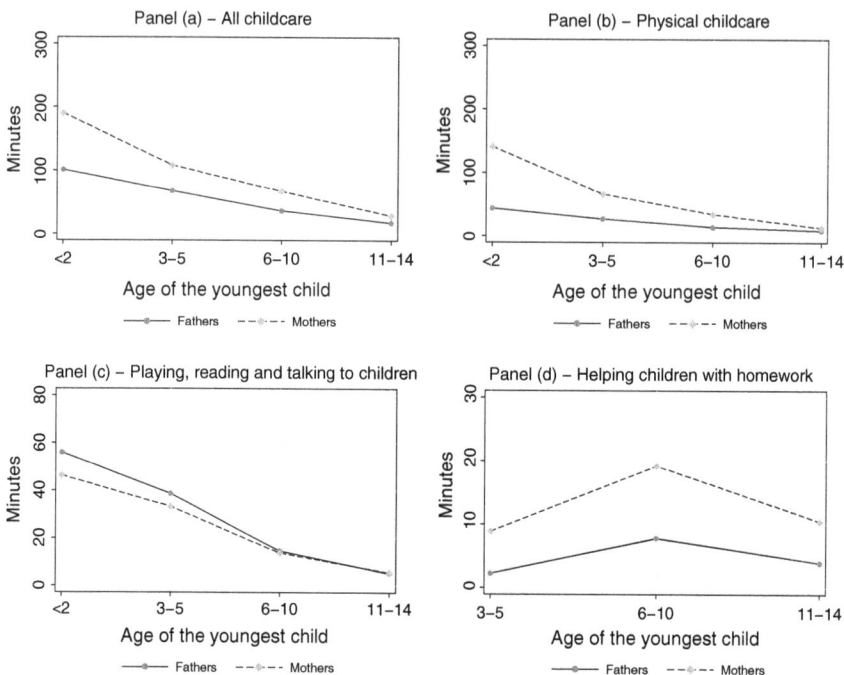

Fig. 3.8 Time on different types of childcare among mothers and fathers aged 20–64. ISTAT TUS 2013–14

minutes decrease among both parents as children grow. The pattern is different for the interactive childcare activities shown in panels (c) and (d): mothers and fathers appear to be similarly engaged in playing with and reading to very young children. It would even appear that fathers are slightly more engaged in interactive childcare than mothers when their children are 2 years old or less, likely because mothers in this stage are more involved in physical care. In contrast, the gender gap emerges once again when it comes to helping school age children with homework (panel (d)). These figures suggest that fathers are more likely to spend time on the more pleasurable parts of childcare while mothers spend more time carrying out the least pleasant and rewarding yet unavoidable tasks.

3.5.3 Adult Care

We now move to consider the third pillar of unpaid domestic work: adult care. According to the Italian Time Use data, this activity is performed by a minority of subjects. During the life stages considered in this volume, only about 5% of women and 3% of men engaged in adult care on the diary day. Caring for an adult is not a routine activity for many households and it is not well captured by time use data. Indeed, among most households, adult care can be considered an extra-ordinary and occasional task. Conversely, for a minority of households it can represent a daily task. As a result, adult care does not appear in daily diaries as frequently as housework and childcare. In light of this, we do not analyse time spent by all individuals in adult care but rather we focus on the percentages of subjects who engaged in adult care on the diary day and report average time on adult care for those who did this activity.

Table 3.2 presents the percentages of subjects who provided adult care on the diary day at various points of the life course and, for those who did, the average care time. Considering that adult care is not an activity that can be carried out by young children, we do not consider women and men under the age of 20. Very few children living in the parental home engage in adult care. We observe a certain degree of participation in adult care, that is, about 5.1% for men and 11% for women, only among children aged 35 and above. In contrast, single, childless women and men aged 20–34 and 35–44 do nearly no adult care. Older singles without children are also unlikely to be involved. Childless women and men in couples are somewhat more engaged: about 3% of men and women aged 35–44 and slightly more in the 45–64 group (3.7% among men and 4.8% among women). Coupled childless women over 65 are more likely to provide adult care (8.7%). On average, young parents are less likely than older ones to provide care. Overall, mothers from 45 to 64 and above 65 are the most involved in adult care (9% and 12% respectively). Table 3.2 also reports the average minutes for those who spend at least 10 min caring for an adult on the diary day. In general, the values suggest that although the activity is performed by a relatively small number of subjects, those who provide care do so for rather long timespans.

3.6 Conclusions

This chapter provided an overview of the data, methods and measures used in the volume. It also offered a descriptive narrative of the allocation of time to housework, childcare and adult care among women and men at different stages of the life course. The chapter descriptively showed that women and men in the sample differ in their average day, with women being much more involved in the domestic sphere than men. The results show that, except among very young children, women do considerably more housework than men throughout the life course. Gender differences emerge among sons and daughters as early as elementary school and

Table 3.2 Adult care time and participation. ISTAT TUS 2013–2014. Unweighted values. Own calculations

	Men				Women			
	All subjects		Doers only		All subjects		Doers only	
	%	N	Min	N	%	N	Min	N
Living in the parental home								
Young adult 20–24	1.8	878	171	16	1.9	918	126	17
Adult 25–34	1.4	1098	125	15	1.1	873	68	10
Adult ≥ 35	5.1	805	75	41	11	584	66	65
Single, no children								
20–34	0	392		0	0	258		0
35–44	0	549		0	0.6	333	100	2
45–64	0.43	922	135	4	1.4	982	101	14
≥ 65	0.39	776	17	3	0.38	2393	83	9
Couple, no children								
20–34	3	197	32	6	3.5	284	31	10
35–44	3.2	277	50	9	3.2	252	109	8
45–64	3.7	1067	71	39	4.8	1463	73	70
≥ 65	4.2	2409	85	100	8.7	1930	81	167
Parents								
20–34	2.3	398	19	9	3	768	15	23
35–44	2	1556	50	31	4.1	1884	29	77
45–64	3.3	3478	45	116	9	3112	44	281
≥ 65	4.7	741	109	35	12	426	85	50

increase during adolescence up to early adulthood (Dotti Sani 2016). This result is striking, as gender differences in housework among children should be minimum due to virtually inexistent differences in time, power and resources (Blood and Wolfe 1960; Brines 1994; Greenstein 2000). This aspect, along with the determinants of children's housework time and participation, will be further addressed in Chap. 4. Gender gaps are also present among childless women and men: single women spend considerably more time on housework than single men. Thus, even in the absence of task specialization, women show a greater propensity to take care of their home than men. One the one hand, women might have higher standards for what it means to have a "clean" and tidy house (Bianchi et al. 2000). On the other hand, more elaborate standards might be requested from Italian women in terms of washing clothes separately, ironing etc. Young men might be less competent in this respect and more likely to outsource such tasks. Gender differences in housework time are even more evident among couples, suggesting that task specialization kicks in and latches on to previous disparities. The gender gap in housework among childless women and men and its determinants will be discussed in Chap. 5. The results also suggested that the largest gender differences are among parents, with mothers doing an overwhelmingly large amount of housework compared to fathers

3.6 Conclusions

(Grunow and Evertsson 2016; Schober 2013). The results for childcare mirror those for housework quite closely. Mothers spend much more time than fathers caring for their children and the gap is larger among younger parents, likely due to the presence of very young children whose care needs are more time consuming and difficult to outsource. The results also show that fathers spend slightly more time than mothers in the most enjoyable child care tasks and less in physical care or helping with homework. These aspects as well as the differences between parents of younger and older children will be addressed in detail in Chaps. 6 and 7. Finally, the chapter illustrated that gender differences are present also among older individuals. Within this age group, single and childless women do less housework than their peers who live with their children and a partner. This suggests that women's large burden of housework is driven not just by higher standards or adherence to traditional gender roles, but also by task specialization. Lastly, our descriptive findings highlight that adult care is carried out by a minority of subjects at the time of the survey, but those who engage do so for relatively long spans of time. More on this aspect will be discussed in the chapter dedicated to elder adults, who are the most likely to devote time to this form of care (Chap. 8).

To summarize, the preliminary results discussed in the chapter indicate that when it comes to the domestic setting, be it housework, childcare or adult care, in all stages of the life course the lion's share of the workload rests on women's shoulders.

References

Álvarez, B., & Miles-Touya, D. (2012). Exploring the relationship between parents' and children's housework time in Spain. *Review of Economics of the Household, 10*(2), 299–318.

Ben-Arieh, A., & Ofir, A. (2002). Time for (more) time-use studies: studying the daily activities of children. *Childhood, 9*(2), 225–248.

Bianchi, S., Milkie, M., Sayer, L., & Robinson, J. (2000). Is anyone doing the housework? Trends in the gender division of household labor. *Social Forces, 79*(1), 191–228.

Billari, F. (2004). Becoming an adult in Europe: A macro (/micro)-demographic perspective. *Demographic Research, 3,* 15–44.

Blood, R., & Wolfe, D. (1960). *Husbands and wives: The dynamics of married living*. New York, NY: Free Press.

Brines, J. (1994). Economic dependency, gender, and the division of labor at home. *American Journal of Sociology, 100*(3), 652–688.

Cunningham, M. (2001). The influence of parental attitudes and behaviors on children's attitudes toward gender and household labor in early adulthood. *Journal of Marriage and Family, 63*(1), 111–122.

Dotti Sani, G. M. (2014). Men's employment hours and time on domestic chores in European countries. *Journal of Family Issues, 35*(8), 1023–1047.

Dotti Sani, G. M. (2016). Undoing gender in housework? Participation in domestic chores by Italian fathers and children of different ages. *Sex Roles, 74*(9–10), 411–421.

Greenstein, T. N. (2000). Economic dependence, gender, and the division of labor in the home: A replication and extension. *Journal of Marriage and Family, 62*(2), 322–335.

Grunow, D., & Evertsson, M. (2016). *Couples' transitions to parenthood*. Cheltenham, UK Northampton, MA, USA: Edward Elgar.

Henz, U. (2006). Informal caregiving at working age: Effects of job characteristics and family configuration. *Journal of Marriage and Family, 68*(2), 411–429.

Hsin, A. (2009). Parent's time with children: Does time matter for children's cognitive achievement? *Social Indicators Research, 93*(1), 123–126.

ISTAT. (1988). *Indagine Multiscopo sulle Famiglie. Uso del Tempo Anno 1988–89*.

ISTAT. (2002). *Indagine Multiscopo sulle Famiglie. Uso del Tempo Anno 2002–2003*.

ISTAT. (2008). *Indagine Multiscopo sulle Famiglie. Uso del Tempo Anno 2008–2009*.

ISTAT. (2013). *Indagine Multiscopo sulle Famiglie. Uso del Tempo Anno 2013–2014*.

Lachance-Grzela, M., & Bouchard, G. (2010). Why do women do the lion's share of housework? A decade of research, *Sex Roles, 63*(11–12), 767–780.

Leve, L. D., & Fagot, B. I. (1997). Gender-role socialization and discipline processes in one-and two-parent families. *Sex Roles, 36*(1–2), 1–21.

Long, J. S., & Freese, J. (2014). *Regression Models for categorical dependent variables using stata* (3rd ed.). College Station, TX: The Stata Press.

Manke, B., Seery, B. L., Crouter, A. C., & McHale, S. M. (1994). The three corners of domestic labor: Mothers', fathers', and children's weekday and weekend housework. *Journal of Marriage and the Family, 56*(3), 657–668.

Neilson, J., & Stanfors, M. (2014). It's about time! Gender, parenthood, and household divisions of labor under different welfare regimes. *Journal of Family Issues*. 0192513X14522240.

OECD. (2017). *OECD family database*. Retrieved October 26, 2016.

Schober, P. S. (2013). The parenthood effect on gender inequality: Explaining the change in paid and domestic work when British couples become parents. *European Sociological Review, 29*(1), 74–85.

Schulz, F., & Grunow, D. (2012). Comparing diary and survey estimates on time use. *European Sociological Review, 28*(5), 622–632.

Stewart, J. (2013). Tobit or not tobit? *Journal of Economic and Social Measurement, 38*(3), 263–290.

Chapter 4
Domestic Work Among Children, Teenagers, and Young Adults

Abstract This chapter focuses on time in the domestic setting among sons and daughters of different ages. The chapter shows that as early as elementary school little girls engage more in domestic work than little boys and spend more time doing chores as well. Such gap continues to increase in adolescence and, by age 20, girls do over two times more housework than boys. The discrepancy is especially evident for typically female activities such as cooking, cleaning and doing the laundry, whereas boys are more involved when it comes to odd jobs. The chapter also shows that, of all the individual and household characteristics that can affect children's domestic work, having a father who engaged in domestic chores is a strong predictor of children's participation. This result is especially evident for boys, suggesting the existence of a gender specific pattern of imitation between fathers and sons. In other words, fathers who are involved in the care of their home and children act as positive role models for their sons. Alternatively, gender ideology might act at the household level as mothers may push both husbands and sons into doing more housework.

Keywords Domestic work · Housework · Children · Teenagers
Young adults · Gender differences · Fathers · Mothers · Fathers' housework
Socialization · Imitation · Life course · Italy · Italian time use survey

4.1 Introduction

This chapter investigates early socialization to domestic chores by studying the allocation of time to and participation in different types of housework among children, teenagers and young adults living with their parents. Focusing on children rather than adults allows gaining important insights into the gendered nature of domestic work. Indeed, time availability and relative resources theories posit that housework is strongly related to endowments—such as time and money—that are distributed differently between adult women and men (Blood and Wolfe 1960; Hiller 1984). According to the theories discussed in Chap. 2, women typically have less economic power to bargain a more equitable division of chores and, conversely, have more available time to perform it since they generally are less involved in the labour market. However, it is problematic to apply such reasoning to children, as there is no reason to believe that little boys should have more economic resources or less free time than little girls. The social construction of gender approach (Brines 1994; Ferree 1990), as well as socialization models (Bandura 1977), therefore, appear more suitable to account for the unequal allocation of housework among children, although they imply that children of both genders adopt (and adapt to) specific gender roles very early in life (see for example Dotti Sani 2016; Platt and Polavieja 2016). By focusing on children's housework behaviour and by exploring its determinants, the analyses offer a more nuanced understanding of the development of gendered behaviour in housework in the traditional Italian context.

The chapter addresses three main questions: (1) to what extent do sons and daughters of different ages engage in overall domestic work and in typically female and gender-neutral tasks? (2) Do parental characteristics such as education and employment affect children's housework? (3) Is paternal involvement in housework associated with boys' and girls' time on and participation in domestic chores? Regarding the latter, the choice of focusing on fathers' and not mothers' participation in domestic chores is motivated by the fact that virtually all Italian mothers engage in housework on a daily basis (Dotti Sani 2012, 2016). Thus, while nearly all children are constantly exposed to maternal participation in domestic chores, fathers' contribution to housework is something not all children experience everyday (Romano et al. 2012). It is therefore a suitable candidate for explaining gender differences in housework among sons and daughters. In other words, we ask whether fathers who *undo gender* (Deutsch 2007) in housework influence the way their sons and daughters participate in domestic chores. Considering that Italy is among the European countries with the lowest levels of societal gender equality (EIGE 2015), studying whether fathers *undo gender* by participating in domestic chores and whether doing so influences their children's behaviour—especially their sons'—is highly relevant.

4.2 Children's Housework Time and Participation: Who Is Doing What?

As discussed in Chap. 3, for the analyses of sons' and daughters' housework we consider six age groups: pre-school children (aged 3–5), primary school children (aged 6–10), middle school children (aged 11–14), high school kids (aged 15–19), young adults (aged 20–24), adults (aged 25–34) and older adults over 35 years old. Moving beyond the description of general housework, Table 4.1 shows the amount of time daughters and sons spend on different housework activities and their participation in these tasks.

Daughters do more housework than sons and participate more frequently in all age groups and all activities, except among pre-school children. As children grow

Table 4.1 Average minutes spent on and participation in domestic chores. Sons and daughters. ISTAT TUS 2013–2014. Unweighted values. Own calculations

	Age groups						
	3–5	6–10	11–4	15–19	20–24	25–34	≥35
	Sons						
Min/day							
Housework	19	24	23	26	40	40	76
Cooking	1.5	3.5	4.9	6.3	12	9.3	18
Washing and cleaning	1.5	4.8	6.8	7.3	9.8	8.9	17
Odd jobs	16	16	12	12	18	22	41
Percent doers							
Housework	28	39	44	43	48	45	59
Cooking	5.2	12	16	20	27	24	32
Washing and cleaning	4	17	24	22	22	17	25
Odd jobs	22	21	17	15	22	26	40
N	519	917	812	986	878	1098	805
	Daughters						
Min/day							
Housework	17	28	39	58	93	112	204
Cooking	2.4	5.4	14	22	33	38	72
Washing and cleaning	2.7	6.9	12	21	35	41	91
Odd jobs	12	16	12	15	25	33	40
Percent doers							
Housework	29	47	59	66	77	80	89
Cooking	7.7	16	33	44	58	60	76
Washing and cleaning	8.2	21	35	41	52	55	73
Odd jobs	17	24	19	21	33	36	47
N	478	899	770	972	918	873	584

older, the gender gap becomes wider because girls progressively engage in housework in greater numbers and for longer periods. For example, the amount of time spent cooking goes from virtually zero among pre-school boys to 18 min among older ones (35 and above). A similar pattern emerges for washing and cleaning the house. Sons' time doing odd jobs increases more with age, going from around 15 min among pre-school boys to about 40 min among adult men. Daughters' housework time increases at a much faster pace: cooking and washing and cleaning go from basically zero in the 3–5 age group to 72 and 91 min per day respectively among daughters aged 35 and older. Time on odd jobs also increases, indicating that it is far from being a chore just for boys. The results for participation in all types of housework are quite similar. Consider cooking: about 16% of girls aged 6–10 cooked on the diary day. For girls aged 11–14 the figure is about 33%, it reaches 44% among girls aged 15–19, it continues to increase and reaches 76% among daughters older than 35. For sons, participation goes from 12% among boys aged 6–10 years old to 32% among men aged 35 and older. Thus, daughters cook much more than sons at all ages. The table shows that they are also more engaged in washing and cleaning, and odd jobs. Thus, it clearly appears that a gendered learning or adaptation process is in place: boys and girls alike are involved in domestic work when they are very young but grow apart as they become older.

4.3 The Correlates of Children's Housework: Family Structure, Parental Education, Working Status and Housework Participation

To study the association between sons' and daughters' housework and household characteristics, we focus on children living with both parents. Doing so is necessary, as it is not possible to evaluate the effect of, for example, paternal participation in housework among children who live only with their mothers. However, removing single parent households implies ignoring important differences in housework behaviour that could occur among children living in different household configurations. Therefore, before moving to the analyses of housework among children in two parent households, we briefly consider how family structure affects housework time.

Table 4.2 shows the distribution of the children in the sample in two-parent versus single parent households. First, we can observe that most of the children in the sample reside with both parents. This is especially evident among younger children (≤ 5 years old): above 90% live with their mothers and fathers. Not surprisingly, the percentage of one parent households increases with the children's age, especially among those who live with their mothers. This likely occurs because mothers are more likely to obtain custody of their children in case of divorce and, for older children, because of women's longer life expectancy. Just a minority of young children lives exclusively with their father. Keeping these differences in mind, it is relevant to point out that sons and daughters who live with one parent spend more time on housework than children living with both parents. For example, regardless of age, sons living with both parents do approximatively half an hour of chores per day. The figure becomes an hour per day if they live with their father and 46 min if, conversely, they reside with their mother. The difference among daughters is even more striking: girls who live with both parents do 68 min/day of general housework while the value reaches 106 min/day if they live only with their mother and 126 min per day if they live with their father. These values must be taken with caution, as they are based on a relatively small number of observations, in particular for what concerns children living with their fathers (140 daughters and 202 sons). However, they provide an important indication about the salience of family structure in children's time on housework. Moreover, these diverging patterns of housework further justify the choice of focusing on children who live in intact families, that represent the most common configuration among Italian households.

Table 4.2 Percentages of household types by age of the child. Sons and daughters living in the parental home. ISTAT TUS 2013–2014. Unweighted values. Own calculations

%	Two-parents	Single father	Single mother
3–5	91.47	0.70	7.82
6–10	88.60	0.99	10.41
11–14	86.73	1.20	12.07
15–19	82.38	2.50	15.12
20–24	81.12	2.84	16.04
25–34	78.23	4.77	17.00
≥35	54.64	7.49	37.87
Total	80.49	2.97	16.53
N	9264	342	1903

To understand to what extent family matters for children's engagement in different types of domestic chores,[1] Tables 4.3 and 4.4 report the results for the multivariate OLS and logistic regressions where time and participation in four types of housework are modelled: general housework (M1), cooking (M2), washing and cleaning (M3) and odd jobs (M4). Each model is run separately for sons and daughters. Starting from absolute time in Table 4.3, the values of the constant confirm that daughters spend more time on all types of chores than sons (Antill et al. 1996; Belloni and Carriero 2008; Bonke 2010; Gager et al. 2009).

Several household variables are included to account for children's time on housework. As can be seen, however, the main predictor is age. Older sons spend more time on general housework, cooking, washing and cleaning and, to a smaller extent, odd jobs, than younger ones. Similarly, age has a strong and positive effect on all four activities among daughters. The coefficients for daughters, however, are considerably larger, indicating that girls more than boys spend progressively more time doing domestic work. As for other characteristics, non-employed sons and daughters spend more time on housework than students and employed subjects, but the result is strongly mediated by age. The effects of maternal education are mostly not statistically significant and small in magnitude, while having a highly educated father reduces the time daughters spend on general housework, cooking and washing and cleaning. This might occur because highly educated fathers do not offload their domestic responsibilities onto their daughters, as they prefer that they invest their time in other, more rewarding activities. Parental employment status is moderately associated with children's time on domestic work but without a clear pattern. The effect of geographical area is rather small, but we do see that daughters in the South and Islands spend more time washing and cleaning and less time on odd jobs than elsewhere. Paternal housework time appears to have a significant effect. In fact, the more time fathers spend on all types of housework, the more time their sons spend as well. Daughters are also affected by their fathers' time on housework, but to a somewhat smaller extent. Overall, the results suggest that while children's age is the strongest predictor of absolute time on housework, paternal

---

[1] In the multivariate models, we exclude the youngest children whose participation rates and time are too low to allow proper comparisons with the other groups.

Table 4.3 Multiple regression models. Dependent variables: daily minutes spent on all housework, cooking, washing and cleaning and doing odd jobs. ISTAT TUS 2013–2014. Unweighted values. Own calculations

	M1		M2		M3		M4	
	All housework		Cooking		Washing & cleaning		Odd jobs	
	Sons	Daughters	Sons	Daughters	Sons	Daughters	Sons	Daughters
Child age (r.c. 6–10)								
11–14	−0.514	10.072*	1.881	8.830***	2.409	5.366*	−4.808	−4.229
	(3.335)	(4.309)	(1.181)	(1.957)	(1.408)	(2.403)	(2.649)	(2.407)
15–19	−3.145	19.010***	2.973**	14.507***	2.311	9.560***	−8.465**	−5.214*
	(3.255)	(4.178)	(1.153)	(1.898)	(1.375)	(2.330)	(2.587)	(2.336)
20–24	7.888	38.833***	8.089***	20.895***	4.698**	16.080***	−4.926	1.748
	(4.029)	(4.770)	(1.427)	(2.166)	(1.701)	(2.661)	(3.200)	(2.666)
25–34	9.341*	50.687***	8.051***	24.021***	4.613*	17.224***	−3.362	9.330**
	(4.606)	(5.799)	(1.631)	(2.633)	(1.945)	(3.238)	(3.659)	(3.241)
≥35	34.410***	99.544***	13.687***	37.581***	9.277***	47.566***	11.441*	14.258**
	(5.726)	(8.259)	(2.028)	(3.750)	(2.418)	(4.609)	(4.548)	(4.612)
Employment status (r.c. Employed)								
Not employed	14.137***	43.522***	3.377**	15.731***	4.343**	18.837***	6.461*	8.924**
	(3.310)	(4.857)	(1.174)	(2.203)	(1.398)	(2.707)	(2.629)	(2.713)
Student	−2.587	−10.811*	3.573*	0.656	0.558	−6.374*	−6.686*	−5.048
	(3.954)	(5.247)	(1.401)	(2.381)	(1.670)	(2.924)	(3.141)	(2.931)
Mother's education (r.c. low ed.)								
Medium ed.	−2.951	−7.551*	0.772	−3.245*	−1.651	−2.499	−2.059	−1.634
	(2.516)	(3.373)	(0.892)	(1.533)	(1.063)	(1.881)	(1.999)	(1.884)
High ed.	2.705	−2.663	1.617	−3.352	−0.124	3.037	1.261	−2.178
	(3.956)	(5.055)	(1.403)	(2.296)	(1.671)	(2.820)	(3.141)	(2.824)

(continued)

4.3 The Correlates of Children's Housework ...

Table 4.3 (continued)

	M1 All housework		M2 Cooking		M3 Washing & cleaning		M4 Odd jobs	
	Sons	Daughters	Sons	Daughters	Sons	Daughters	Sons	Daughters
Father's education (r.c. low ed.)								
Medium ed.	2.582	−5.334	−0.086	−3.801*	2.426*	−5.010**	0.239	3.485
	(2.462)	(3.275)	(0.872)	(1.487)	(1.040)	(1.827)	(1.956)	(1.830)
High ed.	−5.830	−12.371*	−1.287	−4.843*	−0.089	−7.823**	−4.464	0.287
	(3.861)	(5.015)	(1.368)	(2.277)	(1.631)	(2.797)	(3.067)	(2.801)
Mother's employment (r.c. Not employed)								
Employed	−0.044	−1.029	−1.070	−2.398	−1.842*	−0.481	2.771	1.429
	(2.205)	(2.978)	(0.789)	(1.364)	(0.932)	(1.658)	(1.749)	(1.658)
Father's employment (r.c. Not employed)								
Employed	−8.463**	−6.894	−0.137	−0.952	−1.370	2.433	−6.901***	−7.971***
	(2.649)	(3.787)	(0.927)	(1.690)	(1.099)	(2.072)	(2.082)	(2.097)
Geographical area (r.c. North West)								
North East	5.144	4.265	1.198	2.850	3.958**	4.981*	0.026	−3.508
	(3.162)	(4.206)	(1.120)	(1.909)	(1.336)	(2.345)	(2.511)	(2.349)
Centre	−5.902	−6.518	−0.834	−1.514	−0.460	−1.172	−4.614	−4.029
	(3.340)	(4.529)	(1.183)	(2.057)	(1.411)	(2.530)	(2.653)	(2.530)
South	−5.463	5.787	−1.623	1.506	−1.399	8.705***	−2.499	−4.799*
	(2.886)	(3.899)	(1.022)	(1.775)	(1.218)	(2.174)	(2.288)	(2.174)
Islands	−0.415	7.308	1.933	3.923	0.996	9.749***	−3.414	−6.499*
	(3.720)	(5.083)	(1.318)	(2.308)	(1.573)	(2.837)	(2.954)	(2.840)

(continued)

Table 4.3 (continued)

	M1 All housework		M2 Cooking		M3 Washing & cleaning		M4 Odd jobs	
	Sons	Daughters	Sons	Daughters	Sons	Daughters	Sons	Daughters
Day of the week (r.c. weekend)								
Week day	−5.822**	−6.877*	−1.243	−0.583	−0.997	−1.470	−3.613*	−5.045**
	(2.076)	(2.811)	(0.730)	(1.267)	(0.873)	(1.557)	(1.645)	(1.562)
Father's time on domestic work								
All housework	0.103***	0.066***						
	(0.008)	(0.012)						
Cooking			0.100***	0.037*				
			(0.008)	(0.016)				
Washing and cleaning					0.096***	0.058***		
					(0.009)	(0.016)		
Odd jobs							0.105***	0.067***
							(0.008)	(0.008)
Constant	22.002***	42.773***	−1.980	8.487**	2.575	11.915**	21.547***	23.401***
	(5.219)	(6.956)	(1.832)	(3.121)	(2.185)	(3.828)	(4.113)	(3.832)
N	4281	3824	4281	3824	4281	3824	4281	3824
Significance	0.000	0.000	0.000	0.000	0.000	0.000	0.000	0.000

Note: r.c. = reference category. *p < 0.05, **p < 0.01, ***p < 0.001

4.3 The Correlates of Children's Housework ... 57

Table 4.4 Multiple logistic models. Dependent variables: daily participation in all housework, cooking, washing and cleaning and doing odd jobs. ISTAT TUS 2013–2014. Unweighted values. Own calculations

	M1		M2		M3		M4	
	All housework		Cooking		Washing & cleaning		Odd jobs	
	Sons	Daughters	Sons	Daughters	Sons	Daughters	Sons	Daughters
Child age (r.c. 6–10)								
11–14	0.256*	0.472***	0.467**	0.876***	0.587***	0.770***	−0.329*	−0.349**
	(0.107)	(0.107)	(0.153)	(0.126)	(0.132)	(0.119)	(0.135)	(0.132)
15–19	0.154	0.732***	0.680***	1.330***	0.411**	0.928***	−0.612***	−0.350**
	(0.105)	(0.106)	(0.147)	(0.121)	(0.132)	(0.116)	(0.138)	(0.127)
20–24	0.415**	1.169***	1.239***	1.778***	0.580***	1.254***	−0.377*	0.189
	(0.128)	(0.128)	(0.164)	(0.134)	(0.158)	(0.128)	(0.163)	(0.135)
25–34	0.421**	1.441***	1.325***	1.861***	0.379*	1.326***	−0.221	0.291
	(0.147)	(0.164)	(0.187)	(0.157)	(0.184)	(0.152)	(0.181)	(0.161)
≥35	0.883***	1.830***	1.729***	2.175***	0.767***	1.798***	0.257	0.645**
	(0.182)	(0.255)	(0.225)	(0.219)	(0.227)	(0.216)	(0.215)	(0.221)
Employment status (r.c. Employed)								
Not employed	0.383***	0.344*	0.466***	0.195	0.413**	0.429***	0.142	0.384**
	(0.105)	(0.148)	(0.124)	(0.122)	(0.131)	(0.122)	(0.120)	(0.127)
Student	0.210	−0.086	0.521***	−0.118	0.354*	−0.086	−0.378*	−0.220
	(0.125)	(0.150)	(0.151)	(0.130)	(0.155)	(0.130)	(0.158)	(0.143)
Mother's education (r.c. Low ed.)								
Medium ed.	0.044	−0.106	0.054	−0.048	−0.015	−0.065	0.030	−0.010
	(0.080)	(0.090)	(0.102)	(0.089)	(0.100)	(0.087)	(0.099)	(0.097)
High ed.	0.158	0.067	0.049	−0.057	0.110	0.172	0.193	0.057
	(0.125)	(0.135)	(0.156)	(0.135)	(0.150)	(0.132)	(0.154)	(0.144)
								(continued)

Table 4.4 (continued)

	M1		M2		M3		M4	
	All housework		Cooking		Washing & cleaning		Odd jobs	
	Sons	Daughters	Sons	Daughters	Sons	Daughters	Sons	Daughters
Father's education (r.c. Low ed.)								
Medium ed.	0.095	0.004	0.133	−0.194*	0.101	−0.079	0.183	0.096
	(0.078)	(0.088)	(0.099)	(0.087)	(0.097)	(0.085)	(0.096)	(0.093)
High ed.	−0.016	−0.186	−0.017	−0.267*	0.006	−0.151	−0.135	−0.066
	(0.122)	(0.132)	(0.155)	(0.134)	(0.150)	(0.131)	(0.156)	(0.146)
Mother's employment (r.c. Not employed)								
Employed	−0.164*	−0.130	−0.268**	−0.144	−0.327***	−0.047	0.178*	−0.020
	(0.070)	(0.080)	(0.091)	(0.079)	(0.088)	(0.077)	(0.087)	(0.086)
Father's employment (r.c. Not employed)								
Employed	−0.061	−0.300**	0.071	−0.160	0.005	0.008	−0.119	−0.296**
	(0.083)	(0.102)	(0.103)	(0.096)	(0.105)	(0.094)	(0.101)	(0.107)
Geographical area (r.c. North West)								
North East	0.111	0.013	0.208	0.124	0.318**	0.099	−0.148	0.024
	(0.099)	(0.113)	(0.119)	(0.111)	(0.118)	(0.109)	(0.120)	(0.117)
Centre	−0.205	−0.293*	−0.148	−0.141	−0.094	−0.297*	−0.170	−0.193
	(0.105)	(0.120)	(0.131)	(0.120)	(0.132)	(0.119)	(0.127)	(0.129)
South	−0.464***	−0.041	−0.513***	−0.037	−0.191	0.049	−0.359**	−0.249*
	(0.092)	(0.105)	(0.119)	(0.104)	(0.116)	(0.102)	(0.112)	(0.111)
Islands	−0.159	0.031	−0.072	−0.046	−0.059	0.085	−0.291*	−0.419**
	(0.117)	(0.138)	(0.145)	(0.135)	(0.148)	(0.132)	(0.145)	(0.150)

(continued)

4.3 The Correlates of Children's Housework … 59

Table 4.4 (continued)

	M1 All housework		M2 Cooking		M3 Washing & cleaning		M4 Odd jobs	
	Sons	Daughters	Sons	Daughters	Sons	Daughters	Sons	Daughters
Day of the week (r.c. Weekend)								
Week day	−0.013	−0.163*	−0.026	−0.038	0.106	−0.068	−0.162	−0.154
	(0.066)	(0.075)	(0.084)	(0.073)	(0.081)	(0.073)	(0.083)	(0.082)
Father's participation in domestic work								
All housework	0.447***	0.507***						
	(0.076)	(0.081)						
Cooking			0.516***	0.356***				
			(0.082)	(0.074)				
Washing & cleaning					0.423***	0.219**		
					(0.082)	(0.076)		
Odd jobs							0.889***	0.776***
							(0.086)	(0.081)
Constant	−0.863***	−0.143	−2.751***	−1.410***	−2.172***	−1.255***	−1.344***	−1.179***
	(0.174)	(0.197)	(0.213)	(0.185)	(0.209)	(0.180)	(0.209)	(0.195)
N	4281	3824	4281	3824	4281	3824	4281	3824
Significance	0.000	0.000	0.000	0.000	0.000	0.000	0.000	0.000

Note: r.c. = reference category. *$p < 0.05$, **$p < 0.01$, ***$p < 0.001$

behaviour is an important element, indicating that parental behaviour more than parental characteristics, such as education and employment status, matter in shaping children's time on domestic work.

Table 4.4 reports the results for participation in, rather than time on, housework. As can be seen, age remains the predominant factor in accounting for sons' and daughters' housework. Once again, however, the coefficients are larger among daughters. The non-employed and, to a smaller extent, students participate more in chores than their employed peers, but the result is not always statistically significant. As in the case of housework time, parental education and employment status have little if any effect on sons' and daughters' participation. However, having a highly educated father somewhat reduces girls' cooking. Interestingly, having an employed mother reduces participation in general and female typed housework among sons but not among daughters. Geographical area also has an effect, as sons in the South are less likely to engage in general housework, cooking, and odd jobs. No notable difference emerges for daughters.

Moving to fathers' participation, we can see that the chances of sons and daughters engaging in general housework are greater if the father spent at least 10 min on housework on the diary day. Similarly, children are more likely to engage in cooking, cleaning and washing and doing other housework if their father does so. These results suggest that fathers have an important role in shaping their children's participation in housework (Cunningham 2001). The magnitude of the coefficients, however, suggests that the effects vary by the gender of the child. Except when it comes to general housework, the coefficients for sons are larger than the ones for daughters. This suggests that when a father is involved in housework, boys more than girls are affected by his behaviour (Álvarez and Miles-Touya 2012; Penha-Lopes 2006). To get a better understanding of the magnitude of the interaction effects, Fig. 4.1 plots the predicted probabilities for sons and daughters of doing each type of housework conditioning on whether the father did the activity. The predictions are accompanied by 95% confidence intervals and are adjusted by setting all the other variables in the model to the sample means.

The probability that a son does any housework increases from 0.34 if his father did no housework to 0.46 if the father did at least 10 min of housework on the diary day. Daughters' participation goes from 0.59 to 0.69 and the increase is statistically significant. Thus, the results for general housework indicate that children have higher chances of participating in housework if their father participates (Álvarez and Miles-Touya 2012; Penha-Lopes 2006). It is important to recall that the probabilities are derived from the models in Table 4.4 that control for a variety of parental characteristics. This suggests that more than parental characteristics, it is parental and in particular *paternal* behaviour that mostly affects children's behaviour (Evertsson 2006; Gager et al. 2009). The results for cooking are similar: sons whose fathers cooked have a chance of doing so themselves that is 10 percentage points higher than that of sons whose fathers did not (0.22 vs. 0.13). The difference for daughters is smaller, as the probability goes from 0.38 to 0.45. Fathers' example is even more important for sons' when it comes to washing and cleaning: sons whose fathers engaged in this group of activities have a 0.24 chance of doing so

4.3 The Correlates of Children's Housework ...

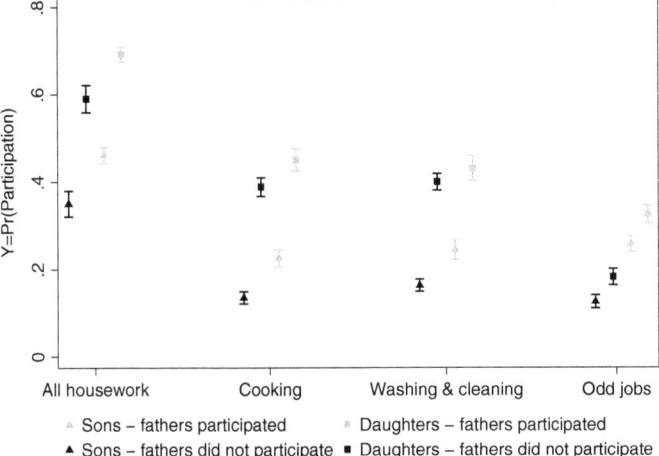

Fig. 4.1 Predicted probabilities and 95% confidence intervals of participating in different types of housework among sons and daughters. ISTAT TUS 2013–2014. Own calculations

themselves versus the 0.16 chance of sons whose fathers did not engage. The difference for daughters is also present but it is much more modest. Finally, fathers influence their children also when it comes to odd jobs but, in this case, gender differences in the effect of paternal participation are much smaller.

4.4 Conclusions

This chapter has investigated the amount of time Italian boys and girls of different age groups spend on different types of housework. It also focused on participation in housework during this stage of the life course. Importantly, the chapter tested whether paternal participation is positively associated with children's participation, and whether boys more than girls are likely to imitate their father's behaviour. Two considerations can be drawn. First, the chapter has provided empirical evidence of a gender gap in housework that is present not just among Italian adults (Bianchi et al. 2014; Dotti Sani 2012), but also among children, teenagers and young adults. The fact that little girls, female teenagers and young women engage in housework more frequently than their male counterparts suggests that time availability and bargaining theories account for only a part of gender inequalities in housework. Indeed, we have no reason to believe that little girls participate in chores more than little boys because they have more free time or less bargaining power: to the contrary, power and time are likely to be equally distributed between genders when children are young (Lundberg 2005). Thus, adherence to traditional gender roles is likely to account, at least in part, for boys' and girls' unequal participation in housework. In other words, Italian children seem to adhere to traditional gender roles and to *do gender* (Deutsch 2007; West and Zimmerman 1987, 2009) in housework just as their parents. Thus, either because they choose to, or because their parents impose it, or perhaps because of the frequency of same-sex interactions between parents and children, Italian boys and girls embrace a rather traditional allocation of housework chores. Unfortunately, with the current data, it is impossible to ascertain which of these three explanations is more likely. Second, the results show that paternal participation in housework has a positive association with children's and young adults' participation. Moreover, it appears that boys more than girls are positively influenced by their father's participation, indicating the presence of a *gender-specific imitation process* previously documented in studies for other Western countries (Álvarez and Miles-Touya 2012; Cunningham 2001; Dotti Sani 2016; Penha-Lopes 2006). This has important implications for the future development of gender inequalities in housework. Indeed, if boys and young men learn to do domestic chores in the parental home because their fathers are *undoing gender* in housework and thus act as a role model towards such behaviour, they might consider housework *a man's thing* and continue to participate in housework as adults (Penha-Lopes 2006). The long term positive consequence of this would likely be a more gender equal division of domestic chores between adult women and men. Lamentably, it is impossible with this data to verify whether the behaviour of sons and daughters will actually be maintained in their transition to adulthood and whether there are long lasting effects of paternal housework participation on men and women's participation in housework as adults. Future research will need to address these issues. Furthermore, additional insights could be gained by exploring whether the results change by sibling composition, for example by considering the number of siblings and gender-mixed vs. single-gender sibship. For space limitations and because of the relatively small sample sizes in each age group, this analysis was omitted in the present chapter, but represents a promising avenue for future studies.

It is important to stress the importance of the 'intergenerational transmission' of gender roles for the future development of societal gender inequalities in a country, Italy, that has overall very low levels of equality between women and men (WEF 2016), where women are underrepresented in the political field (Sundström 2013) and are largely out or at the margins of the labour market (OECD 2016). More relevantly to the present study, Italian women do much more housework and provide more care to family members than women in other Western countries, and men much less (Bianchi et al. 2014; Craig et al. 2010; Hook 2010). Despite some changes in recent years, a large part of Italian households still feature a male breadwinner and a female homemaker, at least at certain stages of the life course (Dotti Sani and Scherer 2017). In such scenario, it becomes evident that young women and men are extremely exposed to gendered patterns of behaviour and they are likely to imitate—at least to some extent—some of their parents' attitudes and behaviours and to inherit part of their values (Bandura 1977; Cichy et al. 2007; Goffman 1977). On top, the reproduction of social inequalities passes in large part through family ties (Black et al. 2005; Kalmijn 1994), especially in a country like Italy, where intergenerational mobility is low. Of course, with the increase in the educational level of boys and girls and women's growing presence in the labour market (Scherer and Reyneri 2008), we would expect gender roles to eventually

4.4 Conclusions

evolve towards greater equality and the sharing of housework (Bolzendahl and Myers 2004; Cichy et al. 2007). Yet, the fact that Italian women currently do the lion's share of housework even when they are employed and highly educated (Dotti Sani 2012), suggests that their children are in large numbers being exposed to a gender traditional division of unpaid work even when paid work is being equally shared between their parents. How this will impact their future housework behaviour is yet to be seen. Indeed, it must be noticed that, even in gender-equal Sweden, one of the countries where the allocation of domestic tasks between partners is closest to being equal (Dotti Sani 2014), little girls spend more time on chores than little boys (Evertsson 2006), suggesting that socialization to traditional gender roles in domestic chores is one among the many factors that contribute to embracing more or less traditional gender roles as adults (West and Zimmerman 1987, 2009). Moreover, it remains to be understood whether fathers could be brought to do more domestic work, for example though specific policies, with the aim of rooting the notion that domestic unpaid work is *a man's thing*.

To wrap up, the role of children's socialization for future gender equality is likely more complex than it appears (Deutsch 2007). However, it might be more effective in the achievement of the societal balance between genders than is usually believed, and therefore needs to be studied in a more comprehensive fashion than single country studies have been able to do so far. In the next chapter, we take a step forward in the life course by focusing on the allocation of time to unpaid domestic work among adult childless women and men who have left the parental home.

References

Álvarez, B., & Miles-Touya, D. (2012). Exploring the relationship between parents' and children's housework time in Spain. *Review of Economics of the Household, 10*(2), 299–318.

Antill, J. K., Goodnow, J. J., Russell, G., & Cotton, S. (1996). The influence of parents and family context on children's involvement in household tasks. *Sex Roles, 34*(3–4), 215–236.

Bandura, A. (1977). *Social learning theory*. Oxford England: Prentice-Hall.

Belloni, C., & Carriero, R. (2008). Il tempo dei bambini [Children's Time]. In Romano, M. C. (Ed.), *I tempi della vita quotidiana. Un approccio multidisciplinare all'analisi dell'uso del tempo* (pp. 175–217). Roma: ISTAT.

Bianchi, S., Lesnard, L., Nazio, T., & Raley, S. (2014). Gender and time allocation of cohabiting and married women and men in France, Italy, and the United States. *Demographic Research, 31*(8), 183–216.

Black, S. E., Devereux, P. J., & Salvanes, K. G. (2005). Why the apple doesn't fall far: Understanding intergenerational transmission of human capital. *The American Economic Review, 95*(1), 437–449.

Blood, R., & Wolfe, D. (1960). *Husbands and wives: The dynamics of married living*. New York, NY: Free Press.

Bolzendahl, C. I., & Myers, D. J. (2004). Feminist attitudes and support for gender equality: Opinion change in women and men, 1974–1998. *Social Forces, 83*(2), 759–789.

Bonke, J. (2010). Children's housework-Are girls more active than boys? *Electronic International Journal of Time Use Research, 7*(1), 1–16.

Brines, J. (1994). Economic dependency, gender, and the division of labor at home. *American Journal of Sociology, 100*(3), 652–688.

Cichy, K. E., Lefkowitz, E. S., & Fingerman, K. L. (2007). Generational differences in gender attitudes between parents and grown offspring. *Sex Roles, 57*(11–12), 825–836.

Craig, L., Mullan, K., & Blaxland, M. (2010). Parenthood, policy and work-family time in Australia 1992–2006. *Work, Employment and Society, 24*(1), 27–45.

Cunningham, M. (2001). The influence of parental attitudes and behaviors on children's attitudes toward gender and household labor in early adulthood. *Journal of Marriage and Family, 63*(1), 111–122.

Deutsch, F. M. (2007). Undoing gender. *Gender and Society, 21*(1), 106–127.

Dotti Sani, G. M. (2012). La divisione del lavoro domestico e delle attività di cura nelle coppie italiane: un'analisi empirica. *Stato e Mercato, 94*(1), 161–192.

Dotti Sani, G. M. (2014). Men's employment hours and time on domestic chores in European countries. *Journal of Family Issues, 35*(8), 1023–1047.

Dotti Sani, G. M. (2016). Undoing gender in housework? Participation in domestic chores by Italian fathers and children of different ages. *Sex Roles, 74*(9–10), 411–421.

Dotti Sani, G. M., & Scherer, S. (2017), Maternal employment: Enabling factors in context. First published January 2017. In *Work, employment and society*, pp. 1–18.

EIGE. (2015). *Gender Equality Index 2015*. European Institute for Gender Equality. www.eige.europa.eu/gender-statistics.

Evertsson, M. (2006). The reproduction of gender: Housework and attitudes towards gender equality in the home among Swedish boys and girls. *The British Journal of Sociology, 57*(3), 415–436.

Ferree, M. M. (1990). Beyond separate spheres: Feminism and family research. *Journal of Marriage and the Family, 50*(4), 866–884.

Gager, C. T., Sanchez, L. A., & Demaris, A. (2009). Whose time is it? The effect of employment and work/family stress on children's housework. *Journal of Family Issues, 30*(11), 1459–1485.

Goffman, E. (1977). The arrangement between the sexes. *Theory and Society, 4*(3), 301–331.

Hiller, D. V. (1984). Power dependence and division of family work. *Sex Roles, 10*(11–12), 1003–1019.

Hook, J. L. (2010). Gender inequality in the welfare state: Sex segregation in housework, 1965–2003. *American Journal of Sociology, 115*(5), 1480–1523.

Kalmijn, M. (1994). Mother's occupational status and children's schooling. *American Sociological Review*, 257–275.

Lundberg, S. (2005). Sons, daughters, and parental behaviour. *Oxford Review of Economic Policy, 21*(3), 340–356.

OECD. (2016). *LMF1.6: Gender differences in employment outcomes*. Retrieved October 8, 2017.

Penha-Lopes, V. (2006). "To Cook, Sew, to Be a Man": The socialization for competence and black men's involvement in housework. *Sex Roles, 54*(3–4), 261–274.

Platt, L., & Polavieja, J. (2016). Saying and doing gender: Intergenerational transmission of attitudes towards the sexual division of labourRepa. *European Sociological Review, 32*(6), 820–834.

Romano, M. C., Mencarini, L., & Tanturri, M. L. (2012). *Uso del tempo e ruoli di genere Tra lavoro e famiglia nel ciclo di vita*. Rome: Istituto Nazionale di Statistica.

Scherer, S., & Reyneri, E. (2008). Come è cresciuta l'occupazione femminile in Italia: fattori strutturali e culturali a confronto. *Stato e Mercato, 83*(2), 183–216.

Sundström, A. (2013). Women's local political representation within 30 European countries: A comparative dataset on regional figures. In *The Quality of Government Institute Working Paper Series* (Vol. 18).

WEF (2016) *The Global Gender Gap Report*. World Economic Forum, Geneva, Switzerland. http://reports.weforum.org/global-gender-gap-report-2016.

West, C., & Zimmerman, D. (1987). Doing gender. *Gender and Society, 1*(2), 125–151.

West, C., & Zimmerman, D. (2009). Accounting for doing gender. *Gender and Society, 23*(1), 112–122.

Chapter 5
Young and Beautiful. Domestic Work Among Childless Women and Men

Abstract This chapter examines the time use patterns of childless women and men living independently or in couples. Women and men at this stage are not expected to be strongly affected by dynamics of time availability, power and resources compared to older individuals and parents. In contrast, our results indicate that gender differences are present among both singles and partnered individuals. Gender differences peak among couples and especially for typically female activities such as cooking, cleaning the house and doing the laundry. The chapter also analyses whether individual characteristics—such as level of education, employment status and area of residence—affect time on and participation in housework. The results largely confirm previous findings: highly educated women do fewer chores than low educated ones and non-employed women do more. Moreover, women in the Southern regions and in the Islands tend to do more housework compared to the Northern area and men less, again confirm previous results on the large cultural differences within the country, with the South being more traditional. Thus, even among younger and, in principle, more modern Italians, women are doing significantly more housework than men.

Keywords Domestic work · Housework · Gender differences · Life course
Italy · Italian time use survey

5.1 Introduction

This chapter focuses on the allocation of time to and participation in housework among relatively young Italian women and men who have left the parental home and are either living on their own or in couples. Drawing on theories of relative resources, time availability and gender ideology discussed in Chap. 2 (Blood and Wolfe 1960; Brines 1994; Ferree 1990; Hiller 1984), the chapter illustrates how women and men with different characteristics (e.g. age, level of education, employment status) have different behaviours in terms of time and participation in housework. The chapter also provides empirical evidence on the division of

© The Author(s) 2018
G. M. Dotti Sani, *Time Use in Domestic Settings Throughout the Life Course*,
SpringerBriefs in Sociology, https://doi.org/10.1007/978-3-319-78720-6_5

domestic chores between partners by focusing on the relative rather than the absolute time spent on housework (Dotti Sani 2014; Knudsen and Wærness 2008). Importantly, women and men in this stage of the life course are likely less affected by dynamics of time availability, power and resources compared to older individuals and especially parents (Anxo et al. 2011). Thus, we expect childless and young women and men to be spending less time on domestic work, compared to older subjects and, for couples, to be sharing housework rather equally. Moreover, we expect individual characteristics to play a minor role in determining the allocation of time to housework, given a relatively egalitarian starting point. As will be shown, these expectations are largely unfulfilled.

5.2 Housework Among Childless Couples: Who Is Doing What?

The relatively young age of the respondents analysed in this chapter—childless adults aged 20–44 living independently or in couples—drives us to expect a relatively gender equal allocation of time to domestic work. Indeed, both women and men are likely to have achieved higher education and be employed (OECD 2016a, b) both elements that reduce housework time and participation. Moreover, they have been socialized in times of greater gender equality compared to previous generations (Inglehart and Norris 2003) and are therefore likely to hold gender egalitarian values in comparison (although we do not directly test this assumption). Table 5.1 reports summary statistics for the groups analysed in this chapter. As can be seen, women of all ages and couple status have much higher education than men, reflecting the increasing levels of education among Italian women as well as possible selection mechanisms behind the timing of home leaving among women and men with different levels of education. In all groups, men are more likely to be employed than women, but differences are small among singles and larger among couples. This suggests that task specialization among partnered women and men is present even before children are born. Still, about 70% of partnered women are employed during this stage of the life course, indicating that gender differences in employment patterns are relatively modest among young Italians. Table 5.1 also shows that the sample is homogenously spread in the five macro-areas. Focusing only on couples, we can see that the distribution of income depicts a rather traditional gender divide as men earn significantly more than their partners: nearly 50% of men earn more or much more than their partner and, on average, about 40% of couples earn approximatively the same amount. Finally, the distribution of marital status by age reflects the well known pattern by which women tend to marry younger than men.

What is the distribution of domestic work in this stage of the life course? Table 5.2 reports the mean time on general housework and a subset of activities that

5.2 Housework Among Childless Couples: Who Is Doing What?

Table 5.1 Summary statistics by age and couple status. Women and men aged 20–44. ISTAT TUS 2013–2014. Unweighted values. Own calculations

	Men				Women			
	Singles		Couples		Singles		Couples	
	20–34	35–44	20–34	35–44	20–34	35–44	20–34	35–44
Level of education (%)								
Low	28	32	26	32	17	18	20	23
Medium	52	45	56	51	50	46	53	46
High	20	24	18	18	33	36	27	31
Employment status (%)								
Employed	84	86	89	90	77	84	71	72
Not employed	16	14	11	10	23	16	29	28
Geographical area (%)								
North West	23	25	32	26	27	21	30	24
North East	19	18	24	24	19	24	25	26
Centre	20	22	16	21	16	24	16	22
South	29	23	17	20	24	20	20	20
Islands	9	10	10	8	10	10	10	10
Division of household income (%)								
Respondent much more			26	31			3	9
Respondent more			21	20			5	7
About the same			43	36			41	31
Respondent less			3	8			21	19
Respondent much less			7	5			30	33
Marital status (%)								
Married	0	0	47	70	0	0	57	70
Not married	100	100	53	30	100	100	43	30
Day of the week								
Weekend	66	64	70	65	66	65	67	68
Weekday	34	36	30	35	34	35	33	32
N	363	421	194	261	249	297	279	234

reflect the most common domestic chores: cooking and meal preparation; cleaning the house; washing clothes, ironing, mending etc.; other odd and non-routine jobs including domestic maintenance, gardening, shopping and household management. As shown already in Chap. 3, large gender differences can be seen in general housework: at all ages, women do more than men. Importantly, gender differences tend to increase with age, with older women doing more housework than younger ones among both singles and couples. These differences are found also in terms of cooking, cleaning the house and washing activities. Clear evidence of task specialization emerges from cooking: women in couples do more than single

Table 5.2 Average minutes and participation in domestic work. Childless women and men aged 20–44. ISTAT TUS 2013–2014. Unweighted values. Own calculations

	Men		Women	
	Min	%	Min	%
Housework				
Singles				
20–34	85	75	137	89
35–44	93	79	161	94
Couples				
20–34	96	75	209	94
35–44	94	75	219	98
Cooking				
Singles				
20–34	32	61	52	78
35–44	36	65	58	80
Couples				
20–34	24	48	80	87
35–44	23	49	86	88
Cleaning				
Singles				
20–34	18	36	44	64
35–44	21	39	52	71
Couples				
20–34	23	40	69	75
35–44	20	35	60	75
Washing				
Singles				
20–34	2.8	6.3	8.2	16
35–44	3.1	7.1	11	25
Couples				
20–34	0.67	3.1	17	29
35–44	0.96	2.3	22	32
Odd jobs				
Singles				
20–34	32	35	33	43
35–44	33	40	40	53
Couples				
20–34	48	47	44	52
35–44	51	52	50	62

women, and men in couples do less than single men. The pattern is evident for both absolute time and percentage of subjects involved. As for cleaning the house, men engage in this task for about 20 min without substantial differences between singles and partnered men, whereas women do more on average (about 50 min) and spend even more time if they are in a couple vs. single. Washing, ironing and mending clothes are activities that take away virtually no time from men. By contrast, young single women spend only 9 min per day on this activity whereas older women in couples reach a maximum of about 22 min, again pointing towards gender specialization among couples. When it comes to odd jobs, gender differences are smaller, suggesting that men's engagement in these activities represents their main contribution to domestic work, as highlighted in previous studies (Treas and Drobnič 2010).

5.3 Determinants of Housework Among Childless Young Adults: What Matters?

Despite being young, with relatively high levels of education, in a stage of life when time and resource constraints should be minimum, women and men display clear gender differences in housework. In this section, we explore the individual and household characteristics that are associated with time on and participation in housework, and with the division of domestic chores among couples.

Starting from absolute time spent on chores, research has shown that level of education, employment status and values are associated with the time women and men spend on housework. In this respect, our data only partially match previous findings. As can be seen from panel (a) in Fig. 5.1, highly educated, single men aged 20–34 do more than low and medium educated ones, whereas highly educated women in the same group do less than their lower educated peers. Among singles aged 35–44, education has basically no effect among men, while it has a moderately negative effect among women. Among couples, education has the expected negative effect among women in both age groups, and a positive effect only among men in the younger group. Overall, these figures indicate that being highly educated strongly reduces housework among women, especially partnered ones, while the effects of education among men are, at best, ambivalent and strongly dependent on other characteristics such as age and partnership status. The results for employment status shown in panel (b) in Fig. 5.1 are more straightforward, as they clearly indicate that employed women and men spend less time on housework compared to non-employed subjects. For women, however, within-gender differences are larger among couples than among singles, again pointing towards the important implications of task specialization between partners.

A third consideration regards cultural differences: women and men living in the Southern regions of the country are more likely to display traditional behaviours in terms of housework (Dotti Sani 2012). Therefore, it is important to consider geographical differences to capture within-country variation in housework behaviour. Panel (c) in Fig. 5.1 shows the average minutes spent on domestic chores by single and coupled women and men in the two age groups in five macro areas: North East, North West, Centre, South and Islands. In all life stages, women in the South and

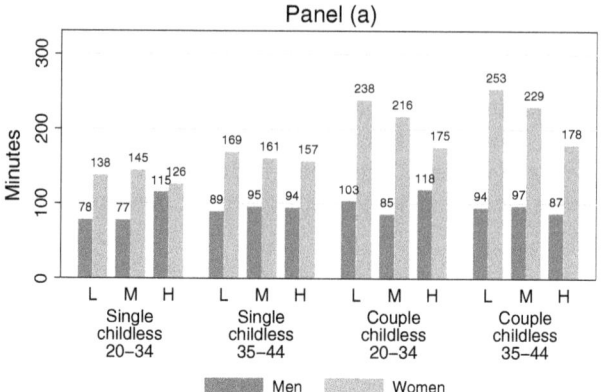

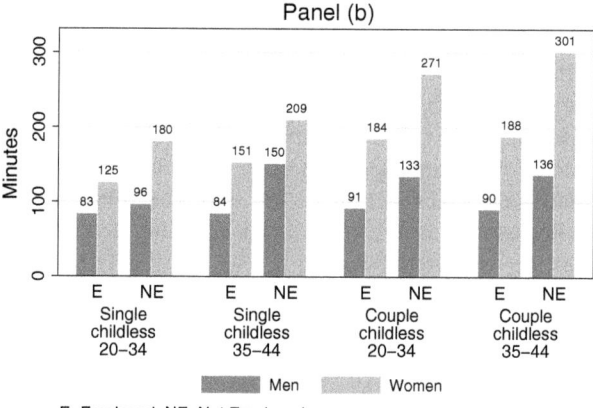

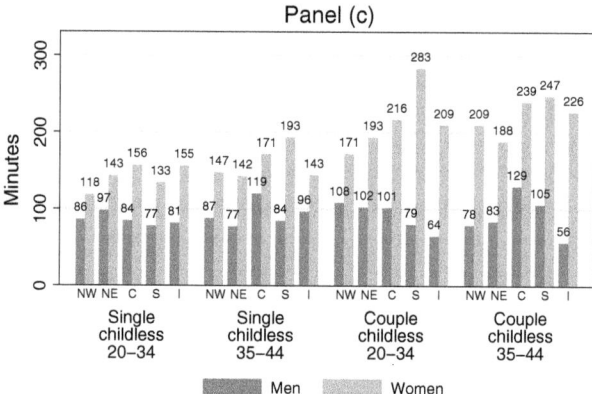

Fig. 5.1 Average minutes of housework among childless adults aged 20–44. ISTAT TUS 2013–2014. Unweighted values. Own calculations. Note: average minutes are conditioned on the stage of the life cycle, gender and education in panel (**a**), employment status in panel (**b**) and geographical macro-area in panel (**c**)

the Islands do much more housework than in other regions, especially among older coupled women, a subgroup that also has a lower likelihood of being employed. In general, there is much more variation among women than among men. Among the former, housework ranges from about 118 min/day among single women aged 20–34 in the North West, to 283 min/day for coupled women aged 20–34 in the South. The absolute difference between the two values is 165 min. Among men, the lowest value is 56 min/day for partnered men aged 35–44 in the Islands and the highest value is 129 min/day, found in the same group but in the central area. The absolute difference is 73 min, half of women's. Compositional differences account for some of the regional variation observed, since female employment rates are much lower in the South of the country than elsewhere. Levels of education are also lower in this area compared to rest of the country. Below we shall discuss the results from the multivariate models, where we can simultaneously keep into account the different individual characteristics that engender variations in housework time.

The panels in Fig. 5.2 show the percentages of subjects who did at least ten minutes of housework on the diary day versus no housework all together. When looking at patterns of housework participation, rather than absolute time, small differences emerge. Participation rates are high among all women, and being highly educated does not reduce housework participation in a meaningful way. The effect of education is rather small among men as well, with higher educated men participating somewhat more among singles. The results conditioning on employment status presented in panel (b) of the figure are similar, as they indicate that employment status makes little difference towards engaging or not in housework. However, participation in housework is high for all women, while men's participation shows greater variability. Lastly, panel (c) in Fig. 5.2 shows the percentages of participation among women and men in the five macro-areas. Participation rates for women are close to or above 90% in all areas. Interestingly, single women living in the South participate somewhat less than their Northern counterparts. Geographical differences are even more evident among men: men in the South and Islands are the least likely to participate in housework, whereas men's participation rates tend to be higher in the Northern regions, especially among singles.

Focusing now on couples, we can grasp a clearer understanding of housework allocation by looking at the *relative* amount of time spent on domestic chores by partners, rather than absolute differences between women and men.[1] Generally

---

[1]The percentages for women and men in Figs. 5.3 do not perfectly sum up to 100 because, to avoid imposing an excessively restrictive sample selection (i.e. both partners being in the same age group), we have also included subjects who are in the considered age group (20–44) but whose partner is above or below the thresholds.

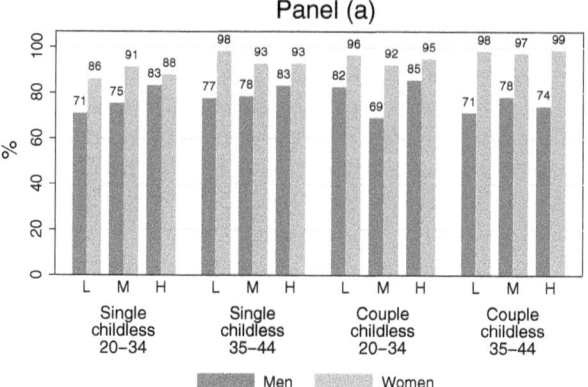
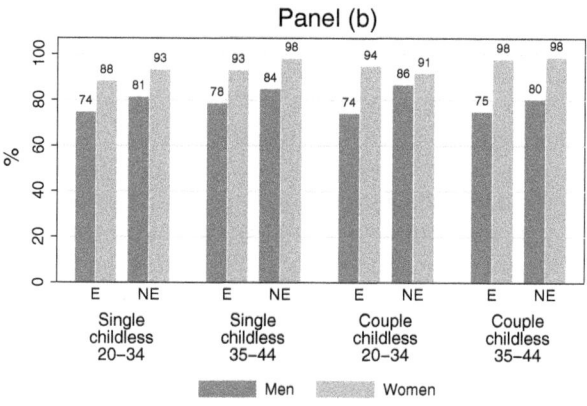
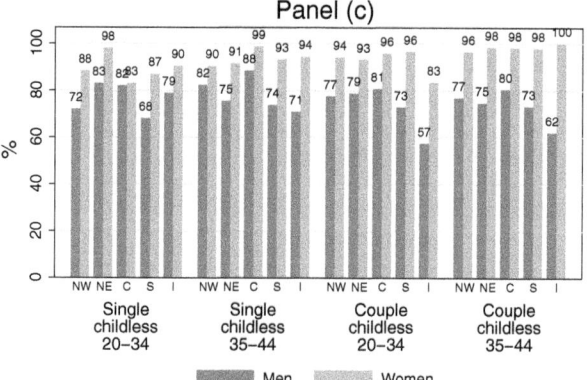

Fig. 5.2 Participation in housework among childless adults aged 20–44. ISTAT TUS 2013–2014. Unweighted values. Own calculations. Note: participation is expressed as percentage of those who did at least 10 min of housework by stage of the life cycle, gender and education in panel (**a**), employment status in panel (**b**) and geographical macro-area in panel (**c**)

5.3 Determinants of Housework Among Childless Young Adults ...

speaking, the division of domestic chores among partners is far from equal in the two age groups considered. In both groups, women do about 70% of the total workload and men about 30%. However, individual characteristics in terms of power and resources count for the division of domestic work. As can be seen from panel (a) in Fig. 5.3, the higher the level of education, the more equitable the division of chores: among the younger households, women who are highly educated do about 61% of the workload compared to 73% among the lower educated. Among the older ones, the difference is smaller: 72% for the lower educated, and 73% for the medium and high educated.

Employment status also matters for the division of housework. As shown in panel (b) in Fig. 5.3, being employed reduces the workload for both women and men in both age groups. Finally, panel (c) shows the difference in the division of domestic chores among women and men in different geographical areas. The results are similar to those discussed earlier about absolute time spent on housework: in both age groups, the division of domestic chores is less equal in Southern Italy and in the Islands, and slightly more equitable in the Centre and Northern area.

To verify simultaneously the effects of different individual characteristics on absolute housework time, participation in housework and the division of domestic chores between partners, we now refer to the results of the multiple regression models reported in Table 5.3. All models are run separately for women and men. This allows us to see whether the effects of education, employment status, geographical location vary by gender.[2] Models 1 and 2 report, respectively, the results for women and men when the dependent variable refers to absolute minutes spent on domestic work. In Models 3 and 4, instead, the dependent variable is housework participation (0 = subject did no housework on the diary day; 1 = subject did at least 10 min of housework on the diary day). Finally, in Models 5 and 6, the dependent variable is the share of domestic work performed by each partner. The variable ranges from 0 to 100, where 0 that stands for the respondent doing no housework and 100 for the respondent doing all the housework on the diary day. In this case, the sample is somewhat smaller as it includes only subjects in couples. All models include the same set of independent variables, that is age group (20–34 and 35–44), level of education (low, medium and high), employment status (employed and not employed), geographical location (North East, North West, Centre, South and Islands), day of the week (weekend and weekday). Being centred on couples only, Models 5 and 6 also include marital status (married vs. not married) and

---

[2]In preliminary analyses gender differences were explicitly modelled by including both women and men in the regression and interacting a dummy variable for gender with all the main predictors of interest. The results indicated that the gender differences in the variables of interest were statistically significant.

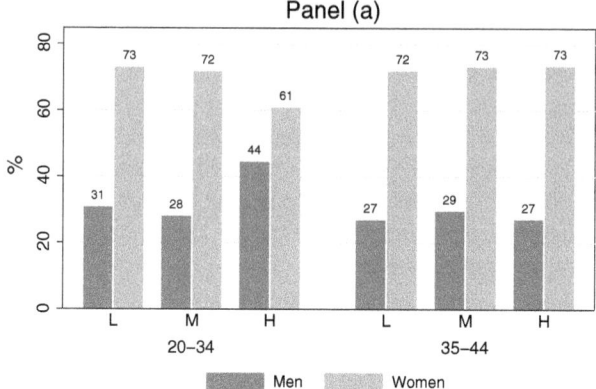
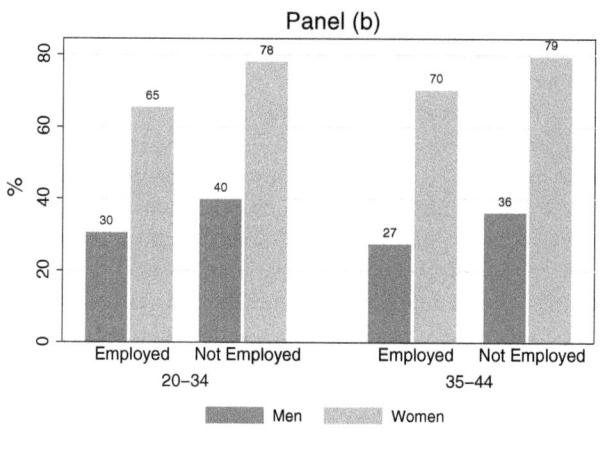
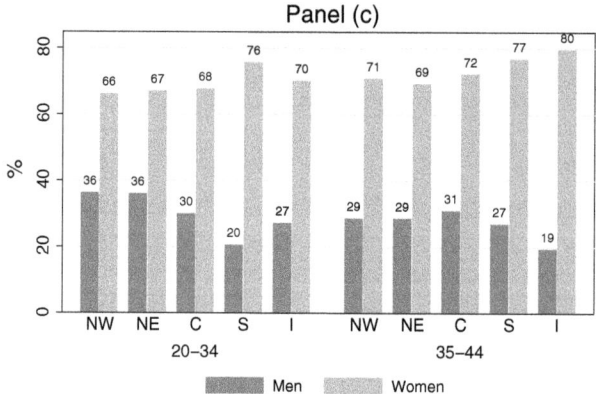

Fig. 5.3 Division of housework expressed in percentages among childless couples aged 20–44. ISTAT TUS 2013–2014. Unweighted values. Own calculations. Note: average shares of housework are conditioned on the stage of the life cycle, gender and education in panel (**a**), employment status in panel (**b**) and geographical macro-area in panel (**c**)

relative income (respondents earn about the same, the respondent earns more than the partner or the respondent earns less than the partner).[3]

Starting from Models 1 and 2, the coefficients indicate a positive effect of age for both women and men, although the result is statistically significant only in the former case. Being members of a couple increases the amount of time spent on housework for both genders. However, the difference for men is rather small and not statistically significant, while the effect is much larger for women (nearly 60 extra minutes per day). The level of education is not a relevant determinant of housework time for men in this stage of the life course, while it is so for women, as high educated ones spend less time on chores than their less educated counterparts. Non-employed men and women spend more time on housework than employed ones (46 and 71 min more respectively). As for geographical area, the models show that even when controlling for important background variables such as education and employment status, women in the South of Italy do more housework than elsewhere (+37 min/day). Not surprisingly, the coefficients for weekdays are negative and significant for both women and men, indicating that more housework is done on weekends.

In Models 3 and 4, the dependent variable taps participation in housework for men and women respectively. Many of the predictors are non-significant, indicating that the individual level variables included in the models do not account for housework participation as well as they did for housework time. Among men, the only exceptions are employment status and region of residence. In contrast, none of the predictors shows a statistically significant association with the outcome among women, with the exception of age group and couple status. The result is not surprising, considering the very high percentage of women involved in domestic chores every day.

Finally, Models 5 and 6 report the results for the division of chores between partners. In this case, age group is not statistically significant. In contrast, highly educated women and men share chores with their partners more than less educated ones, but the result is significant only for men. In relative terms, once again, we find that men in the South and Islands do less housework and women more. However, the coefficients are not statistically significant. Lastly, cohabitation compared to marriage is associated with a lower share of housework among women and a higher one among men, whereas the partner who earns the highest amount does a smaller share of chores, in line with relative resource theory.

---

[3]Due to the relatively small number of observations in some response categories, the variable has been recoded from the original one presented in Table 5.1.

Table 5.3 Multiple regression models. Dependent variables: minutes of housework (Modes 1 and 2), participation in housework (Models 3 and 4), and division of housework between partners (Models 5 and 6). ISTAT TUS 2013–2014. Unweighted values. Own calculations

	Model 1	Model 2	Model 3	Model 4	Model 5	Model 6
	OLS	OLS	Logit	Logit	OLS	OLS
	Men	Women	Men	Women	Men	Women
Age 35–44 (r.c. 20–34)	4.955	18.825*	0.107	0.721**	−1.700	4.395
	(5.811)	(7.868)	(0.137)	(0.265)	(2.520)	(2.287)
In couple (r.c. Not in a couple)	7.164	58.503***	−0.129	0.706**		
	(6.020)	(7.911)	(0.141)	(0.269)		
Level of education (r.c. Low ed.)						
Medium ed.	−1.065	−2.163	0.009	−0.334	0.680	0.962
	(6.698)	(10.572)	(0.155)	(0.373)	(2.831)	(2.961)
High ed.	13.936	−22.892*	0.345	−0.305	7.831*	−4.358
	(8.361)	(11.446)	(0.206)	(0.399)	(3.659)	(3.272)
Not employed (r.c. Employed)	46.008***	71.471***	0.584**	0.283	8.764*	6.797*
	(8.702)	(9.676)	(0.226)	(0.333)	(4.453)	(2.788)
Geographical area (r.c. North West)						
North East	0.500	8.577	0.020	0.384	1.059	−1.821
	(8.501)	(11.166)	(0.202)	(0.369)	(3.349)	(3.118)
Centre	18.156*	29.907*	0.355	0.372	0.960	−1.193
	(8.554)	(11.780)	(0.218)	(0.391)	(3.599)	(3.356)
South	−8.934	37.496**	−0.402*	0.091	−4.752	2.510
	(8.331)	(11.734)	(0.190)	(0.361)	(3.694)	(3.415)
Islands	−17.310	3.015	−0.522*	−0.076	−7.934	2.031
	(10.870)	(14.557)	(0.241)	(0.428)	(4.887)	(4.445)
Week day (r.c. Weekend)	−24.550***	−23.554**	−0.003	0.326	−8.166**	8.057***
	(6.079)	(8.247)	(0.144)	(0.281)	(2.619)	(2.401)
Not married (r.c. Married)					5.606*	−5.238*
					(2.636)	(2.433)
Relative income (r.c. Same income)						
Income > partner					−6.525*	−8.981*
					(2.605)	(3.923)
Income < partner					3.688	2.594
					(4.342)	(2.518)
Constant	85.870***	126.334***	1.129***	2.011***	32.231***	66.362***
	(8.524)	(13.015)	(0.200)	(0.417)	(4.108)	(3.906)
N	1239	1058	1239	1058	419	469
Significance	0.000	0.000	0.000	0.000	0.000	0.000

Note: r.c. = reference category. *p < 0.05, **p < 0.01, ***p < 0.001

5.4 Conclusions

This chapter has focused on housework time and participation among a group of subjects, childless young women and men, who were expected to be relatively egalitarian in their management of domestic chores. Due to their young age and their childless status, these individuals should carry the torch of gender equality. And yet, the results show that housework is strongly gender unequal even among these subjects, as women do more housework than men and they engage more often in it. Moreover, the findings suggest that a strong task specialization is in place, as gender differences in housework are larger among couples than singles. When it comes to personal characteristics, the results confirm that highly educated women spend less time on housework than low educated ones (Blair and Lichter 1991; Dotti Sani 2012; Greenstein 2000), whereas the results for men are less clear cut. Employment status and geographical area are also associated with housework time, suggesting that individual characteristics are important drivers of housework behaviour even among this group. Personal characteristics matter less when it comes to participation rates. Regardless of the level of education, nearly 90% of women engage in housework on the diary day. Employment status is also weakly associated with the percentage of housework doers. The division of domestic chores among partners is also far from equal in both age groups. Overall, women do about 70% of the total housework. Here though, power and resources do account for individual differences. For example, women do a lower share of housework if they are higher educated and employed.

In sum, this chapter showed that despite relatively similar levels of time, resources and power, Italian young women and men are quite traditional in their relationship with housework. Regardless of age and partnership status, women do considerably more housework than men and are more likely to engage in domestic work on the diary day. Moreover, while both women and men increase their time on housework as they grow older and enter a union, such increase is much larger for women, indicating that gender specialization is an important component of the domestic puzzle. Hence, against the initial expectations that among the younger subjects we would observe a more egalitarian allocation of housework, the chapter shows that rooted notions of traditional gender behaviour and roles dominate (Brines 1994; Ferree 1990). In the next chapter, we focus on a stage of the life course that is renowned for its even stronger gendered patterns of behaviour: parenthood.

References

Anxo, D., Mencarini, L., Pailhé, A., Solaz, A., et al. (2011). Gender differences in time use over the life course in France,Italy, Sweden, and the US. *Feminist Economics, 17*(3), 159–195.

Blair, S. L., & Lichter, D. T. (1991). Measuring the division of household labor: Gender segregation of housework among American couples. *Journal of Family Issues, 12*(1), 91–113.

Blood, R., & Wolfe, D. (1960). *Husbands and wives: The dynamics of married living*. New York, NY: Free Press.

Brines, J. (1994). Economic dependency, gender, and the division of labor at home. *American Journal of Sociology, 100*(3), 652–688.

Dotti Sani, G. M. (2012). La divisione del lavoro domestico e delle attività di cura nelle coppie italiane: un'analisi empirica. *Stato e Mercato, 94*(1), 161–192.

Dotti Sani, G. M. (2014). Men's employment hours and time on domestic chores in European countries. *Journal of Family Issues, 35*(8), 1023–1047.

Ferree, M. M. (1990). Beyond separate spheres: Feminism and family research. *Journal of Marriage and the Family, 50*(4), 866–884.

Greenstein, T. N. (2000). Economic dependence, gender, and the division of labor in the home: A replication and extension. *Journal of Marriage and Family, 62*(2), 322–335.

Hiller, D. V. (1984). Power dependence and division of family work. *Sex Roles, 10*(11–12), 1003–1019.

Inglehart, R., & Norris, P. (2003). *Rising tide: Gender equality and cultural change around the world*. Cambridge: Cambridge University Press.

Knudsen, K., & Wærness, K. (2008). National context and spouses' housework in 34 countries. *European Sociological Review, 24*(1), 97–113.

OECD. (2016a). *LMF1.6: Gender differences in employment outcomes*. Retrieved August 8, 2017.

OECD. (2016b). *OECD Education at a glance: OECD indicators 2016*. Retrieved September 11, 2017.

Treas, J., & Drobnič, S. (2010). *Dividing the domestic: Men, women, and household work in cross-national perspective*. Stanford: Stanford University Press.

Chapter 6
Parenthood and Domestic Work: A Never-Ending Workload

Abstract This chapter focuses on parents of children up to 14 years old. According to previous literature, during this life stage gender inequalities in housework are the most acute. The findings show that virtually all mothers do at least 10 min of housework on the diary day, against approximatively 75% of fathers. The results for typically female tasks are even more extreme and reveal just how much Italian parents specialize in terms of home production, with women bearing most of the responsibility. The findings also show that mothers spend more time taking care of their children than fathers. An interesting result in this respect is that mothers are mostly responsible for the routine care and for helping children with homework, whereas fathers are more likely to undertake the most enjoyable part: playing with their children. Finally, the chapter engages with adult care, revealing that this activity is not very common in this age group and shows only minor gender differences in this respect.

Keywords Domestic work · Housework · Childcare · Adult care
Children · Gender differences · Parents · Fathers · Mothers · Motherhood
Fatherhood · Life course · Italy · Italian Time Use Survey

6.1 Introduction

This chapter focuses on the allocation of time to and participation in housework, childcare and adult care among Italian parents whose children are 14 years old or younger. Becoming a parent is an exceptional event that deeply impacts people's lives. It does so in a variety of ways, not just by changing women's and men's habits, behaviours and lifestyles (Evertsson and Boye 2016), but also by modifying their attitudes (Baxter et al. 2015; Katz-Wise et al. 2010). Some authors even suggest that becoming a parent has long-term effects on the brain structure of new mothers (Hoekzema et al. 2017). Among the behavioural outcomes that are well documented is the fact that the allocation of time to domestic work (both housework and childcare) is less gender equal among parents than among childless women and men. Such a phenomenon has been observed not just in cross-sectional studies but

© The Author(s) 2018
G. M. Dotti Sani, *Time Use in Domestic Settings Throughout the Life Course*, SpringerBriefs in Sociology, https://doi.org/10.1007/978-3-319-78720-6_6

also longitudinally, suggesting that even women and men with an egalitarian division of housework switch to gender-traditional behaviour when they become parents (Grunow and Evertsson 2016; Schober 2013). The Italian TUS does not allow making such kind of inference. However, the descriptive analyses in Chap. 3 provided interesting insights by showing that housework time is considerably higher among mothers than among fathers and childless women and men. Moreover, childcare time is strongly affected by the age of the children, with mothers being more engaged in physical care when children are young and in helping with homework when they are older.

In this chapter, we pursue a more fine-grained description of parents' time on housework, childcare and adult care by focusing on the sub-components of domestic work and by exploring to what extent relatively young children affect their parents' time on housework. Moreover, we explore whether and to what extent individual characteristics, such as level of education and employment status, moderate the effect of children's presence on the different components of housework. The chapter draws on theories of relative resources, time availability and gender ideology discussed in Chap. 2 (Blood and Wolfe 1960; Brines 1994; Ferree 1990; Hiller 1984), as well as theories of class differentiation to account for childcare time (Dotti Sani and Treas 2016; Hays 1996; Lareau 2000).

6.2 Parents' Time on Housework

Table 6.1 reports the summary statistics for the sample of subjects used in this chapter. For analytical purposes, we subset the parents in three age groups: 20–34, 35–44 and 45–64. As expected, most mothers and fathers are married and only a minority have a high level of education. On average, mothers are slightly better educated than fathers. Parents appear to be less educated compared to the childless individuals analysed in the previous chapter, indicating that the timing of parenthood varies by level of education, as suggested by previous studies (Billari 2004). Differently from the childless group once more, mothers have considerably lower chances of being employed in all three age groups. As a reflection of this, nearly 70% of fathers declare being the main earners and only about 23% of couples have an equal earning balance. These two pieces of information are important when it comes to the allocation of time to domestic work and even more so when it comes to the division of housework between partners.

How much time do these mothers and fathers spend on the different components of housework? Table 6.2 reports the average time spent by mothers and fathers whose children are 14 or younger doing general housework, cooking, cleaning, washing and doing odd jobs. The table also reports the percentages of subjects who spent at least 10 min on each sub-activity on the diary day. As seen in Chap. 3, virtually all mothers engage in general housework on the diary day. The average amount of time is considerably high, as it goes beyond 300 min/day among mothers aged 45–64. Fathers' participation is around 74% and average time is considerably lower than mothers'.

6.2 Parents' Time on Housework

Table 6.1 Summary statistics. Fathers and mothers aged 20–64 whose children are 14 or younger. ISTAT TUS 2013–2014. Unweighted values. Own calculations

	Fathers			Mothers		
	20–34	35–44	45–64	20–34	35–44	45–64
Age of the youngest child %						
0–2	61	32	7	56	22	2
3–5	27	28	14	28	26	7
6–10	10	29	38	13	36	37
11–14	2	11	40	3	17	54
Number of children (mean)	1.4	1.7	2	1.5	1.8	2
Marital status %						
Married	80	87	91	83	88	93
Not married	20	13	9	17	12	7
Level of education %						
Low	44	39	40	40	29	32
Medium	46	44	41	45	48	47
High	10	16	19	16	24	21
Employment status						
Employed	87	91	91	42	64	60
Not employed	13	9	9	58	36	40
Area of residence %						
North west	23	22	24	22	23	24
North east	19	23	23	21	23	22
Centre	14	17	15	15	17	16
South	32	28	27	31	28	26
Islands	12	10	11	11	9	11
Relative income %						
Respondent more	68	67	66	8	10	11
About the same	22	22	22	18	24	22
Respondent less	10	11	11	74	66	67
Day of the week %						
Weekend	71	64	64	68	63	65
Weekday	29	36	36	32	37	35
N	387	1476	1299	758	1678	726

Gender differences in the sub-components of housework are also evident. Fathers are more likely to contribute to cooking ($\sim$50%) and odd jobs ($\sim$50%), although the time spent on odd jobs is more than twice the time spent cooking. Around 35% of fathers did some cleaning activity on the diary day, averaging at most 20 min, and virtually none gave a contribution to doing the laundry or other related activities. In contrast, over 90% of mothers cooked on the diary day and did so for a considerable amount of time ($\sim$2 h). Nearly 90% of mothers also engaged in some house-cleaning activity for about an hour and a half. Nearly one out of two mothers did the laundry or ironed, averaging another 30 min. Finally, mothers did

Table 6.2 Minutes on and participation in domestic work. Mothers and fathers aged 20–64 whose children are 14 or younger. ISTAT TUS 2013–2014. Unweighted values. Own calculations

	Fathers		Mothers	
	Min.	%	Min.	%
Housework				
20–34	85	72	263	99
35–44	91	74	269	99
45–64	102	77	307	98
Cooking				
20–34	20	44	120	96
35–44	24	50	115	96
45–64	23	48	123	95
Cleaning				
20–34	18	32	85	86
35–44	23	37	91	87
45–64	21	36	102	89
Washing				
20–34	0.41	2.1	23	40
35–44	0.6	2.4	26	42
45–64	0.64	2.3	35	48
Odd jobs				
20–34	47	44	35	48
35–44	44	44	37	51
45–64	57	56	47	59

odd jobs too: about 53% of mothers engaged in this mixed type of chores, averaging close to 40 min.

Overall, the table clearly illustrates that, among parents, it is mothers who bear the largest responsibility for domestic work. Interestingly, older parents tend to do more housework than younger ones. This might occur because younger parents also have younger children that require more childcare time, thus leaving less time for other domestic work. To further investigate this issue, Fig. 6.1 shows predicted minutes[1] on three types of activities (cooking, a combination of cleaning and washing,[2] and odd jobs) conditioning on the age of the youngest child for mothers and fathers respectively. The amount of time spent on domestic work is higher among mothers of older children, though not always in a statistically significant way. Nonetheless, we can observe that mothers of children in the 11–14 age category spend more time cooking and cleaning and washing than mothers of infants. A similar pattern emerges for odd jobs, which range from about 35 min if the youngest child is an infant to 50 min if the youngest child is a teenager. In contrast,

---

[1]The predicted values were calculated starting from a linear model where we regress housework time on gender, age of the youngest child and an interaction between the two variables.

[2]For this and the following analyses we combined washing and cleaning in the same category since men's time and participation in this area is limited.

6.2 Parents' Time on Housework

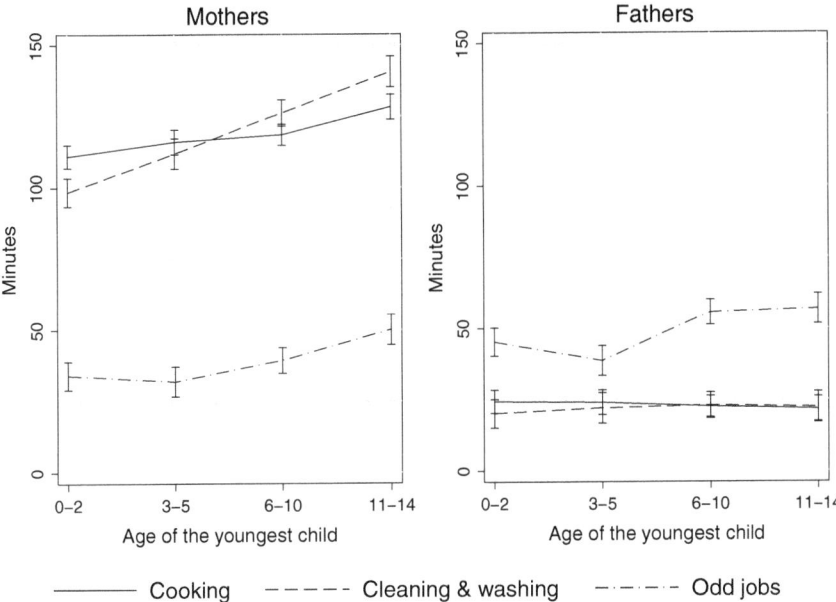

Fig. 6.1 Predicted minutes of housework among mothers and fathers aged 20–64 whose children are 14 or younger. ISTAT TUS 2013–2014. Own calculations

the amount of time spent by fathers on the three types of housework does not vary significantly by age of the youngest child. Overall, the results highlight that children's age has a stronger impact on mothers' time than on fathers', suggesting that gender inequalities in housework actually *increase over time.*

We now move to the multivariate analyses of parents' time on the different subcomponents of housework. Table 6.3 shows the results from a multivariate linear regression where the three subcomponents of domestic work are used as dependent variables. Considering the large differences between mothers' and fathers' time on housework, the models are run separately by gender. Starting from mothers, we can observe that age has a moderate and positive effect on all three groups of activities but, in most cases, it is not statistically significant. Having a child aged 11–14, instead, has a positive and significant effect on all three activities, therefore suggesting that it is the age of the children, more than the age of the mother, that affects domestic work. The number of children is also an important predictor of time spent cooking and washing and cleaning, but not doing odd jobs. Cohabiting mothers spend less time on all three activities than married ones, but the difference is not statistically significant. Such a result contrasts previous findings according to which married couples are more attached to traditional roles and division of labour (Batalova and Cohen 2002; Baxter et al. 2008; Bianchi et al. 2014). The level of education is a very important predictor of mothers' housework time. Higher education has an especially strong effect in reducing time spent cooking and washing and cleaning (Dotti Sani 2012; Sullivan et al. 2014).

Table 6.3 Multiple regression models. Dependent variables: daily minutes spent cooking, cleaning and washing, and doing odd jobs. ISTAT TUS 2013–2014. Own calculations

	Mothers			Fathers		
	Cook	Clean and wash	Odd jobs	Cook	Clean and wash	Odd jobs
Age class (r.c. 20–34)						
35–44	0.695	6.813	2.565	3.629	3.287	−2.789
	(3.363)	(4.237)	(2.801)	(2.230)	(2.819)	(4.829)
45–64	2.144	13.673*	6.259	3.182	0.097	6.350
	(4.479)	(5.642)	(3.731)	(2.519)	(3.184)	(5.454)
Age of the youngest child (r.c. 0–2)						
3–5	3.164	9.554*	−1.674	0.286	2.636	−6.935
	(3.632)	(4.575)	(3.026)	(1.972)	(2.492)	(4.269)
6–10	5.042	20.467***	4.555	−1.794	3.437	7.851
	(3.658)	(4.607)	(3.047)	(1.960)	(2.477)	(4.243)
11–14	11.134*	29.613***	13.682***	−1.956	3.835	6.634
	(4.338)	(5.464)	(3.613)	(2.257)	(2.853)	(4.887)
N° children	9.228***	12.382***	−1.480	0.411	2.188	1.391
	(1.628)	(2.051)	(1.356)	(0.885)	(1.118)	(1.915)
Not married (r.c. married)	−2.720	−8.830	−1.468	0.537	−3.806	−7.560
	(3.846)	(4.845)	(3.203)	(2.106)	(2.662)	(4.559)
Level of education (r.c. Low ed.)						
Medium ed.	−12.547***	−9.168*	1.067	1.951	1.537	0.846
	(2.900)	(3.653)	(2.415)	(1.484)	(1.876)	(3.214)
High ed.	−19.949***	−17.987***	2.336	9.086***	6.168*	−4.360
	(3.691)	(4.649)	(3.074)	(1.995)	(2.521)	(4.318)
Not employed (r.c. employed)	38.771***	32.572***	13.950***	6.464**	12.431***	35.249***
	(2.914)	(3.671)	(2.427)	(2.433)	(3.075)	(5.267)
Geographical area (r.c. north west)						
North east	−6.060	0.418	0.408	2.272	3.729	3.030
	(3.632)	(4.576)	(3.026)	(1.982)	(2.505)	(4.290)
Centre	−2.265	1.111	−1.339	−0.807	−4.037	4.449
	(3.955)	(4.982)	(3.295)	(2.163)	(2.734)	(4.683)
South	15.203***	14.299**	0.870	−9.676***	−9.806***	−7.769
	(3.504)	(4.414)	(2.919)	(1.897)	(2.398)	(4.107)
Islands	5.610	27.946***	−2.192	−6.461**	−7.119*	3.971
	(4.571)	(5.757)	(3.807)	(2.493)	(3.151)	(5.398)

(continued)

Table 6.3 (continued)

	Mothers			Fathers		
	Cook	Clean and wash	Odd jobs	Cook	Clean and wash	Odd jobs
Relative income (r.c. same income)						
Respondent earns more than partner	0.246 (4.653)	−0.453 (5.861)	0.281 (3.876)	−7.922*** (1.644)	−3.813 (2.078)	2.780 (3.559)
Respondent earns less than partner	2.600 (3.192)	9.824* (4.021)	1.464 (2.659)	5.307* (2.520)	6.907* (3.185)	0.465 (5.456)
Week day (r.c. weekend)	1.539 (2.548)	−5.884 (3.210)	−3.900 (2.123)	−5.099*** (1.394)	−12.260*** (1.762)	−27.249*** (3.018)
Constant	84.764*** (5.648)	59.032*** (7.114)	28.314*** (4.704)	26.879*** (3.165)	21.038*** (4.001)	49.380*** (6.853)
N	3162	3162	3162	3162	3162	3162
Significance	0.000	0.000	0.000	0.000	0.000	0.000

Note r.c. = reference category. $*p < 0.05$, $**p < 0.01$, $***p < 0.001$

Predictably, mothers do much more of the three activities if they are not employed, and the differences are always statistically significant (Brayfield 1992; Gough and Killewald 2011; Hiller 1984). Reflecting results from the previous chapters, area of residence is a strong predictor of domestic work, with mothers doing much more cooking and cleaning and washing activities in the South and in the Islands. This again reflects previous findings regarding the large cultural differences that characterise the country (Dotti Sani 2012; Romano et al. 2012). In contrast, how much a mother earns relative to her partner has barely an effect on the amount of time she spends on the three activities, although mothers spend a little more time cleaning and washing if they earn less than their partner.

Fathers' results mirror those of mothers but tend to be of smaller magnitude. Age group, age and number of children and marital status have no effect on fathers' time on the three activities. Level of education positively affects fathers' housework time when it comes to cooking and washing and cleaning, but only among the highly educated. As the literature on time availability predicts, non-employed fathers spend more time on all three activities, but the effect is larger for odd jobs. This could indicate that odd jobs result more appealing to men, in particular when it comes to certain do-it-yourself activities, which would explain why non-employed fathers spend more time on this group of activities (Szinovacz 2000). The results for area of residence also mirror those of mothers, albeit with a smaller magnitude: fathers spend less time cooking and cleaning and washing in the South and Islands. Finally, relative earned income matters for what concerns fathers' cooking and washing and cleaning, as they do somewhat more if they earn less than the partner. Moreover, fathers do considerably less housework on the weekday, especially when it comes to odd jobs, again suggesting that this group of activities could be considered a hobby, at least in part.

Having focused on absolute time spent on the various subcomponents of domestic work, we now move to the way parents *share* housework, that is, we look at the percentage of chores that each parent performs relative to the couple's total housework and we analyse what individual characteristics affect the division of domestic labour. Table 6.4 reports the percentage of general housework, cooking, cleaning and washing and odd jobs performed by fathers and mothers of children 14 or younger divided in three age groups. Across age groups, mothers do about 77% of the general housework load and fathers the remaining 23%. The situation for cooking and washing and cleaning is even more gender-imbalanced, as mothers' contribution surpasses 80%. The division of odd jobs is more egalitarian, with parents being equally likely to perform these tasks. An interesting consideration is that the division of domestic chores is slightly more equal in the older age groups. This likely occurs because children are older in these groups and thus mothers' workload is somewhat smaller.

What characteristics account for the division of different types of domestic work among Italian parents of young children? Table 6.5 reports the results from several generalized linear models where the dependent variables represent the share that partners did of each task. The variables range from 0, indicating that the respondent spent no time on that specific chore on the diary day and the partner did all of it, while 1 means the respondent did all the work and the partner none. In addition to the independent variables included in the previous models, we now add the partner's level of education. In line with relative resource theory, this variable along with relative earned income is expected to play an important role now that the outcome is *relative rather than absolute* time on housework. Starting from mothers, demographic variables have no impact on the share of domestic chores performed. Similarly, the number of children and being married versus cohabitating does not

Table 6.4 Percentage contribution to domestic work. Mothers and fathers aged 20–64 whose children are 14 or younger. ISTAT TUS 2013–2014. Unweighted values. Own calculations

		General housework	Cooking	Cleaning and washing	Odd jobs
		Fathers			
20–34	%	22.51	15.14	14.02	51.46
	N	387	381	354	244
35–44	%	23.31	17.89	15.74	46.65
	N	1463	1446	1358	980
45–64	%	24.42	16.18	14.13	52.27
	N	1289	1267	1220	975
		Mothers			
20–34	%	78.14	84.28	85.60	51.48
	N	754	747	693	483
35–44	%	76.06	82.51	85.12	50.81
	N	1665	1636	1549	1146
45–64	%	75.05	83.42	84.71	48.37
	N	720	711	690	570

6.2 Parents' Time on Housework

Table 6.5 Multiple generalized linear models: dependent variable: share of domestic work. Mothers and fathers aged 20–64 whose children are 14 or younger. ISTAT TUS 2013–2014. Unweighted values. Own calculations

	Mothers			Fathers		
	Cook	Clean and wash	Odd jobs	Cook	Clean and wash	Odd jobs
Age class (r.c. 20–34)						
35–44	0.046	0.175	0.037	0.194	0.083	−0.129
	(0.137)	(0.150)	(0.127)	(0.169)	(0.182)	(0.156)
45–64	−0.013	0.055	−0.090	0.157	−0.015	0.143
	(0.185)	(0.197)	(0.163)	(0.191)	(0.205)	(0.173)
Age of the youngest child (r.c. 0–2)						
3–5	0.106	−0.011	0.101	−0.062	0.038	−0.077
	(0.144)	(0.159)	(0.136)	(0.142)	(0.157)	(0.135)
6–10	0.164	−0.029	0.018	−0.123	0.068	−0.028
	(0.145)	(0.159)	(0.136)	(0.142)	(0.154)	(0.133)
11–14	0.281	0.183	0.156	−0.211	−0.084	−0.178
	(0.179)	(0.195)	(0.158)	(0.170)	(0.185)	(0.152)
N° children	0.049	0.022	−0.082	−0.077	−0.042	0.058
	(0.069)	(0.074)	(0.059)	(0.068)	(0.073)	(0.059)
Not married (r.c. married)	−0.041	0.103	0.087	0.050	−0.093	−0.068
	(0.148)	(0.168)	(0.144)	(0.147)	(0.167)	(0.144)
Not employed (r.c. employed)	0.842***	0.689***	0.440***	0.183	0.404*	0.718***
	(0.129)	(0.137)	(0.105)	(0.179)	(0.180)	(0.163)
Level of education (r.c. low ed.)						
Medium ed.	−0.143	−0.050	0.108	0.114	0.079	0.172
	(0.135)	(0.144)	(0.112)	(0.121)	(0.130)	(0.106)
High ed.	−0.299+	−0.239	0.218	0.306+	0.272	0.077
	(0.168)	(0.181)	(0.152)	(0.163)	(0.177)	(0.152)
Partner's level of education (r.c. low ed.)						
Medium ed.	−0.083	−0.033	−0.121	0.300*	0.205	0.003
	(0.122)	(0.130)	(0.106)	(0.132)	(0.141)	(0.111)
High ed.	−0.204	−0.161	0.013	0.517**	0.452*	−0.020
	(0.163)	(0.177)	(0.153)	(0.164)	(0.177)	(0.149)
Geographical area (r.c. north west)						
North east	−0.094	−0.050	0.044	0.118	0.061	−0.008
	(0.135)	(0.145)	(0.132)	(0.135)	(0.144)	(0.131)
Centre	0.108	0.150	−0.010	−0.132	−0.195	0.002
	(0.153)	(0.167)	(0.144)	(0.152)	(0.166)	(0.144)
South	0.515***	0.547***	0.126	−0.662***	−0.706***	−0.267*
	(0.150)	(0.160)	(0.129)	(0.148)	(0.158)	(0.128)
Islands	0.234	0.452*	−0.247	−0.374*	−0.605**	0.108
	(0.192)	(0.214)	(0.166)	(0.191)	(0.213)	(0.166)

(continued)

Table 6.5 (continued)

	Mothers			Fathers		
	Cook	Clean and wash	Odd jobs	Cook	Clean and wash	Odd jobs
Relative income (r.c. same income)						
Income > partner	−0.143	−0.605***	−0.275	−0.509***	−0.363**	−0.236*
	(0.166)	(0.173)	(0.169)	(0.115)	(0.127)	(0.113)
Income < partner	0.234⁺	0.132	0.086	0.047	0.312⁺	−0.146
	(0.120)	(0.134)	(0.118)	(0.167)	(0.176)	(0.169)
Week day (r.c. weekend)	0.163	0.401***	0.810***	−0.168	−0.398***	−0.826***
	(0.105)	(0.118)	(0.092)	(0.105)	(0.117)	(0.093)
Constant	0.969***	1.119***	−0.494*	−1.367***	−1.483***	0.336
	(0.230)	(0.249)	(0.215)	(0.244)	(0.262)	(0.226)
N	3094	2932	2199	3094	2932	2199
Significance	0.000	0.000	0.000	0.000	0.000	0.000

Note r.c. = reference category. ⁺$p < 0.10$, *$p < 0.05$, **$p < 0.01$, ***$p < 0.001$

affect the division of housework labour. Highly educated mothers share cooking and washing and cleaning with their partners more than low educated ones, but the coefficients are not statistically significant. The results for employment status show that non-employed mothers do more cooking and washing and cleaning in relative terms than the employed ones (80% vs. 90%). They also contribute more to odd jobs. The results for geographical area are also in line with our expectations: mothers in the South and Islands do more relative housework than in other regions of the country, doing respectively 89% and 86% of the cooking against 81% in the North East, for example. Considering the partners' characteristics, we can notice that fathers' education is negatively associated with the outcome, meaning that the higher the fathers' level of education the lower the share of housework performed by the mother. The coefficients, however, are not statistically significant. The expectations for relative earned income are partially fulfilled: mothers who earn more than their partners do less chores than mothers whose earnings equal the partners'. The results, however, are statistically significant only for cleaning and washing, with mothers doing 77% when they earn more than their partners and 88% when they earn less.

The results for fathers closely reflect those for mothers, so we only mention few discrepancies. Similar to mothers, fathers' level of education is positively associated with their share of domestic chores. Furthermore, non-employed fathers contribute more to cleaning and washing and odd jobs than employed ones. The level of education of the partner has a strong and positive effect on the father's share of cooking and cleaning and washing. Specifically, fathers who are partnered to a highly educated woman do 19% of the cooking and 17% of the washing and cleaning compared to 11 and 12% of those partnered to a low educated woman. This finding speaks to the importance of women's education in getting their partners to share chores more equally. It could also relate to our finding in Chap. 4

6.2 Parents' Time on Housework

according to which fathers' participation in housework has a positive effect on sons' participation, as mothers might be able to get not only their husbands but also their sons to do more housework. Finally, fathers who earn more than their partner do significantly less cooking, washing and cleaning and odd jobs than those who earn the same amount.

Another aspect to consider in the division of chores within couples is their work-family arrangement, that is, the way partners allocate their time and resources to the spheres of work and home. Figure 6.2 shows the proportion of general housework done by mothers and fathers who are, respectively, the main earners of their household; members of a dual earner couple; members of a no earner couple; the dependent partner. The predicted values are obtained from a generalized linear model like the ones discussed earlier. Apart from gender and work-family arrangement, the model also controls for some socio-demographic variables such as age group, the age of the youngest child, the number of children, marital status, the level of education of both partners, area of residence and day of the week. The predicted values are adjusted for all the above by setting the covariates at the sample mean. Not surprisingly, all mothers, regardless of the work-family arrangement, in relative terms do much more housework than fathers. However, interesting gender differences emerge. Among mothers, being the main earner entails a significant reduction in the share of housework compared to being the dependent partner, and also compared to being in dual earner and no earner households. In contrast, among fathers there is little difference between being the main earner, in a dual earner couple or in a no earner one, whereas there is quite a large difference between being in one of these three and being the dependent partner. In other words, fathers who are not employed and rely on their partner for

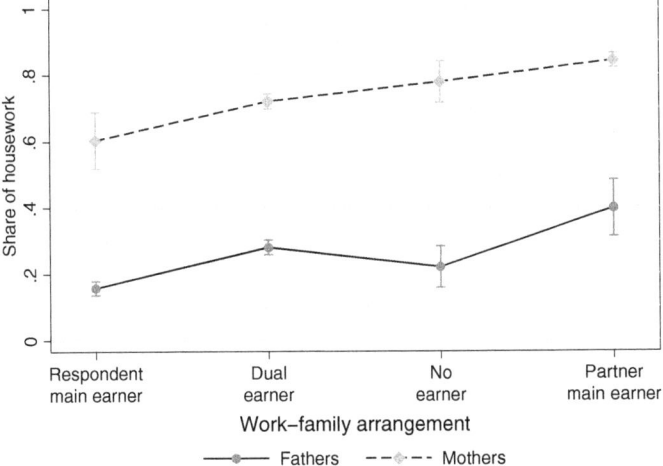

Fig. 6.2 Predicted values with 95% confidence intervals of the share of housework among mothers and fathers aged 20–64 whose children are 14 or younger. ISTAT TUS 2013–2014. Own calculations

income display a much more egalitarian division of chores (doing about 40% of it) compared to fathers in other household types. A note of caution is required here as the number of fathers who are economically dependent on their partners is very small. For this reason, we cannot keep into account the fact that this group might be composed by very different men: those who are involuntarily non-employed as well as those who have chosen a non-traditional division of tasks, a distinction that could lead to valuable insights. However, these results suggest that in dual earner households the division of chores is far from equal, despite similar dedication to paid work by both partners. In contrast, fathers engage more in housework when they are not economically providing for their family. Even so, they are far from being the main providers of domestic work, as happens to mothers who are economically dependent. This confirms once again the existence of large disparities in the way Italian mothers and fathers share responsibilities for their home.

In the following sections, we shall discuss the other two main pillars of domestic work—childcare and adult care—which are likely to be quite demanding in this stage of the life course.

6.3 Childcare and Adult Care

Chapter 3 provided a descriptive overview of childcare time among parents of different ages. Now, we focus on parents of young children to evaluate what individual and household characteristics are associated with the absolute time mothers and fathers spend on different types of childcare and how childcare is divided between parents. The section also investigates adult care in this stage of the life cycle.

Starting from childcare, Table 6.6 reports average time on each subcomponents of childcare for mothers and fathers in three age groups and overall. Recall that, contrary to the figures presented in Chap. 3, these values are calculated on a sub-sample of parents of children age 14 or younger, an age span where intensive, time consuming childcare is required. Focusing first on all childcare, mothers' time nearly doubles fathers' time ($\sim$97 min/day vs. $\sim$60 min/day across all age groups) and mothers' participation is also greater ($\sim$80% vs. $\sim$60%). Moreover, the table indicates that time on and participation in childcare activities is higher among younger parents and decreases with parents' age, likely due to older parents having older children.

The data show that mothers are also the main providers of physical care for their children. While this is evident in all age groups, it is especially notable among parents below age 35, where mothers do over three times the amount of childcare that fathers do: 100 min/day versus 32 min/day. Unlike physical care, that decreases with the age of the parents, helping children with homework becomes more time consuming as parents (and evidently children) grow older. However, it is once again mothers who are the main responsible for this task, as they spend more time on it and in greater numbers. The one big exception to the general rule of

6.3 Childcare and Adult Care

Table 6.6 Minutes spent on and participation in childcare. Mothers and fathers aged 20–64 whose children are 14 or younger. ISTAT TUS 2013–2014. Unweighted values. Own calculations

	Fathers		Mothers	
	Min.	%	Min.	%
All childcare				
20–34	81	75	141	91
35–44	67	65	101	81
45–64	36	45	49	65
Physical childcare				
20–34	32	46	100	87
35–44	28	46	64	74
45–64	14	27	25	53
Helping with homework				
20–34	1.4	1.6	5.6	8.8
35–44	3.8	5.4	12	17
45–64	5.5	7.6	15	21
Interactive childcare				
20–34	47	59	36	49
35–44	35	45	25	44
45–64	17	28	9.3	24

N Fathers: 20–34: 387; 35–44: 1476; 45–64: 1299

N Mothers: 20–34: 758; 35–44: 1678; 45–64: 726

mothers being the main care provider is interactive care, i.e. playing with and reading to children, as it is fathers in all age groups, rather than mothers, that spend more time in this activity. In the two younger groups, fathers spend at least 10 min per day more than mothers playing with and reading to their children.

To further illustrate the differences in childcare time among parents with different characteristics, Tables 6.7 and 6.8 report the results for a set of multivariate regressions where the dependent variables are, respectively, the absolute time on and the participation in each subcomponent of childcare among fathers and mothers respectively. Starting from fathers, age has basically no impact on any type of childcare. In contrast, fathers of older children spend less time on physical and interactive care and are less likely to engage in these activities, but spend more time and are more involved in helping children with homework. Another relevant predictor of physical care and homework help is fathers' level of education. Highly educated fathers spend more time on physical childcare and are more likely to engage in this activity compared to low educated ones (Dotti Sani and Treas 2016; Guryan et al. 2008): a highly educated father on average spends nearly 30 min on physical care and has a 50% chance of engaging in this activity on the diary day. A low educated father spends only 19 min on physical care and has a 30% chance of doing this activity. Education also enhances participation in helping with homework, but the magnitude of the effect is rather small. In contrast, fathers' education has no impact on interactive care time. Surprisingly, employment status is not associated with time and participation in the three activities, whereas the

Table 6.7 Multiple linear and logistic regression models. Dependent variables: minutes spent on and participation in physical childcare, helping with homework and interactive childcare. Fathers aged 20–64 whose children are 14 or younger. ISTAT TUS 2013–2014. Unweighted values. Own calculations

	Physical care		Homework		Interactive care	
	OLS	Logit	OLS	Logit	OLS	Logit
Age class (r.c. 20–34)						
35–44	3.738	0.272*	0.891	0.756	3.324	0.006
	(2.788)	(0.125)	(1.211)	(0.441)	(2.792)	(0.127)
45–64	−1.570	−0.072	1.712	0.866	2.908	0.023
	(3.149)	(0.144)	(1.368)	(0.455)	(3.154)	(0.146)
Age of the youngest child (r.c. 0–2)						
3–5	−16.581***	−0.354**	−0.216	0.358	−16.859***	−0.460***
	(2.464)	(0.109)	(1.070)	(0.324)	(2.468)	(0.110)
6–10	−27.975***	−1.136***	5.121***	1.502***	−40.356***	−1.460***
	(2.450)	(0.112)	(1.064)	(0.283)	(2.454)	(0.114)
11–14	−31.966***	−1.846***	1.093	0.679*	−49.331***	−2.498***
	(2.821)	(0.144)	(1.226)	(0.327)	(2.826)	(0.153)
N° children	0.698	−0.008	0.590	0.131	−7.489***	−0.416***
	(1.106)	(0.053)	(0.480)	(0.098)	(1.107)	(0.057)
Not married	−2.829	−0.225	−1.895	−0.598	2.177	−0.108
(r.c. married)	(2.632)	(0.123)	(1.143)	(0.341)	(2.637)	(0.123)
Level of education (r.c. low ed.)						
Medium ed.	4.843**	0.379***	2.956***	0.656***	3.587	0.155
	(1.855)	(0.089)	(0.806)	(0.183)	(1.858)	(0.090)
High ed.	10.293***	0.794***	1.516	0.514*	4.409	0.091
	(2.493)	(0.117)	(1.083)	(0.235)	(2.497)	(0.120)
Not employed	0.576	−0.181	1.074	−0.027	5.724	−0.194
(r.c. employed)	(3.041)	(0.150)	(1.321)	(0.318)	(3.046)	(0.150)
Geographical area (r.c. north west)						
North east	1.593	−0.062	−0.028	−0.158	−4.700	−0.021
	(2.477)	(0.116)	(1.076)	(0.233)	(2.481)	(0.119)
Centre	−0.296	−0.149	0.713	0.112	−1.775	−0.204
	(2.703)	(0.127)	(1.174)	(0.239)	(2.708)	(0.131)
South	−6.218**	−0.441***	0.442	−0.010	−7.202**	−0.196
	(2.371)	(0.113)	(1.030)	(0.215)	(2.375)	(0.115)
Islands	−8.321**	−0.578***	−1.538	−0.451	−8.583**	−0.206
	(3.116)	(0.152)	(1.354)	(0.329)	(3.122)	(0.151)
Relative income (r.c. same income)						
Income > partner	−3.594	−0.127	−1.853*	−0.379*	−1.026	−0.051
	(2.055)	(0.097)	(0.893)	(0.174)	(2.058)	(0.099)
Income < partner	2.483	0.201	−3.002*	−0.815*	−0.868	−0.098
	(3.150)	(0.149)	(1.368)	(0.340)	(3.155)	(0.153)

(continued)

Table 6.7 (continued)

	Physical care		Homework		Interactive care	
	OLS	Logit	OLS	Logit	OLS	Logit
Week day (r.c. weekend)	−9.749***	−0.133	−0.012	0.244	−10.176***	−0.039
	(1.742)	(0.084)	(0.757)	(0.159)	(1.745)	(0.085)
Constant	44.161***	0.244	0.383	−4.705***	71.705***	1.407***
	(3.956)	(0.183)	(1.719)	(0.524)	(3.963)	(0.191)
N	3162	3162	3162	3162	3162	3162
Significance	0.000	0.000	0.000	0.000	0.000	0.000

Note r.c. = reference category. $*p < 0.05$, $**p < 0.01$, $***p < 0.001$

geographical differences that emerged for housework are also found for childcare. Indeed, men in the South and in the Islands spend significantly less time on physical childcare and playing with children, while no differences emerge for homework. Relative income has no notable effect on childcare time. Finally, in line with time availability theories, fathers spend less time on childcare on weekdays, but the differences are not always statistically significant.

Table 6.8 displays the results for mothers. The reductions in care time associated with having older children are much larger compared to fathers, reflecting the different care patterns discussed in the descriptive analyses. The association between mothers' level of education and time on childcare is strong and significant for most types of care (Dotti Sani and Treas 2016). For example, a highly educated mother spends 74 min on physical care while a low educated one 57 min. Highly educated mothers are also more likely to engage in homework and interactive care, but the educational gradient is smaller. Differently from fathers, employment status influences mothers' childcare: non-employed mothers spend more time on all types of care and are more likely to engage in childcare altogether. The differences, however, are of relatively small magnitude. For example, an employed mother spends about 60 min on physical care a day, and a non-employed one about 70. Chances of participating in physical care are 82% for the non-employed and 76% for the employed. Differences in terms of geographical area do not emerge strongly among mothers. The only significant effects that emerges concerns interactive care, as mothers in the South spend less time on and participate less in this activity.

To better illustrate the results regarding the association between parents' education and childcare, Table 6.9 shows the predicted values for time on and participation in all three types of childcare. Higher educated fathers spend more time on all types of care compared to less educated ones. However, the differences in terms of minutes are not very large, especially when it comes to homework and interactive care time. In contrast, the proportion of fathers who engage in care, mostly physical care, increases notably with education. This suggests that time constraints are similar among fathers with varying degrees of education, perhaps impeding them to spend a lot of time caring for their children. Nonetheless, the educational gradient for participation in physical care is evident (18 percentage

Table 6.8 Multiple linear and logistic regression models. Dependent variables: minutes spent on and participation in physical childcare, helping with homework and interactive childcare. Mothers aged 20–64 whose children are 14 or younger. ISTAT TUS 2013–2014. Own calculations

	Physical care		Homework		Interactive care	
	OLS	Logit	OLS	Logit	OLS	Logit
Age class (r.c. 20-34)						
35–44	4.626	0.057	2.625	0.312	3.294	0.383***
	(3.321)	(0.148)	(1.437)	(0.162)	(1.961)	(0.106)
45–64	0.149	−0.013	3.806*	0.377*	0.121	0.159
	(4.422)	(0.171)	(1.913)	(0.192)	(2.611)	(0.147)
Age of the youngest child (r.c. 0-2)						
3–5	−73.254***	−1.146***	5.126***	0.917***	−11.864***	−0.463***
	(3.586)	(0.205)	(1.551)	(0.197)	(2.118)	(0.110)
6–10	−104.528***	−2.316***	14.438***	1.722***	−31.523***	−1.430***
	(3.611)	(0.194)	(1.562)	(0.187)	(2.132)	(0.116)
11–14	−124.351***	−3.438***	5.257**	0.966***	−37.938***	−1.981***
	(4.283)	(0.209)	(1.853)	(0.214)	(2.529)	(0.147)
N° children	−1.951	−0.135*	1.422*	0.185**	−5.294***	−0.229***
	(1.608)	(0.060)	(0.696)	(0.063)	(0.949)	(0.054)
Not married (r.c. married)	−0.326	−0.057	−2.778	−0.384*	0.748	−0.213
	(3.797)	(0.159)	(1.643)	(0.193)	(2.242)	(0.121)
Level of education (r.c. low ed.)						
Medium ed.	4.558	0.345**	2.666*	0.265*	2.214	0.196*
	(2.863)	(0.106)	(1.238)	(0.120)	(1.690)	(0.094)
High ed.	16.708***	0.690***	2.762	0.215	4.766*	0.369**
	(3.644)	(0.143)	(1.576)	(0.157)	(2.152)	(0.118)
(continued)						

6.3 Childcare and Adult Care

Table 6.8 (continued)

	Physical care		Homework		Interactive care	
	OLS	Logit	OLS	Logit	OLS	Logit
Not employed (r.c. employed)	9.455**	0.410***	5.630***	0.525***	3.454*	0.136
	(2.877)	(0.110)	(1.245)	(0.120)	(1.699)	(0.094)
Geographical area (r.c. north west)						
North east	1.214	−0.028	−2.274	−0.200	0.222	0.047
	(3.586)	(0.137)	(1.551)	(0.149)	(2.118)	(0.115)
Centre	−4.276	−0.176	−2.836	−0.503**	−0.228	−0.129
	(3.905)	(0.148)	(1.689)	(0.170)	(2.306)	(0.126)
South	−0.184	−0.045	−1.145	−0.319*	−9.087***	−0.429***
	(3.460)	(0.131)	(1.497)	(0.140)	(2.043)	(0.113)
Islands	−2.020	0.129	−0.454	−0.445*	−9.579***	−0.515***
	(4.513)	(0.177)	(1.952)	(0.191)	(2.665)	(0.149)
Relative income (r.c. same income)						
Income > partner	−1.842	0.190	1.742	0.282	0.024	0.141
	(4.594)	(0.172)	(1.987)	(0.201)	(2.713)	(0.150)
Income < partner	4.976	0.204	2.084	0.231	1.391	0.151
	(3.152)	(0.118)	(1.364)	(0.142)	(1.861)	(0.103)
Week day (r.c. weekend)	1.089	0.508***	4.491***	0.646***	0.435	0.195*
	(2.516)	(0.098)	(1.088)	(0.102)	(1.486)	(0.082)
Constant	127.392***	2.486***	−6.309**	−3.903***	51.278***	0.485**
	(5.576)	(0.253)	(2.412)	(0.275)	(3.292)	(0.180)
N	3162	3162	3162	3162	3162	3162
Significance	0.000	0.000	0.000	0.000	0.000	0.000

Note r.c. = reference category. $*p < 0.05$, $**p < 0.01$, $***p < 0.001$

Table 6.9 Predicted minutes spent on and participation in three subcomponents of childcare. Fathers and mothers aged 20–64 whose children are 14 or younger. ISTAT TUS 2013–2014. Own calculations

	Minutes				Participation			
	Low	Medium	High	$\Delta_{(high-low)}$	Low (%)	Medium (%)	High (%)	$\Delta_{(high-low)}$
Father								
Physical care	23.1	27.72	31.74	8.64	33	42	51	18
Homework	2.86	6.66	5.21	2.35	0.40	0.80	0.70	0.3
Interactive care	27.24	31.05	32.05	4.82	38	41	40	0.2
Mothers								
Physical care	51.98	58.84	74.62	22.65	66	71	77	11
Homework	8.99	10.94	10.52	1.52	14	17	16	0.2
Interactive care	21.49	23.42	25.42	3.93	37	41	44	0.7

points difference between high vs. low educated). The educational gradient in participation is evident for mothers as well (11 percentage point difference between the high and the low educated) and, as mentioned, highly educated mothers invest significantly more time on physical care than less educated ones. Education is also important for time spent playing with children and for participation in this activity. These results suggest that time with children, regardless of the activity, is more valued among higher than lower educated parents, who plausibly have greater opportunities to spend time with their children and different parenting styles (England and Srivastava 2013; Sayer et al. 2004).

To further explore cultural differences in childcare, Fig. 6.3 reports the predicted minutes (upper panels) and predicted participation expressed as percentages (lower panels) in physical childcare, homework and interactive care for mothers and fathers residing in the five macro-areas considered. Fathers in the Southern regions and the Islands spend somewhat less time on and are less likely to participate in physical childcare than elsewhere. Mothers' time and participation are similar across regions. As for homework, geography matters little among fathers and mothers alike. Finally, in all regions fathers spend more time playing with children than mothers, while participation is similar for both genders. However, both participation and time are clearly higher among parents in the Northern regions.

Our final considerations regard the way parents share childcare. Table 6.10 reports the share of each type of childcare performed by mothers and fathers in the three age groups. The results closely mirror those presented up to here, as they indicate that fathers are more likely to share interactive care than physical care and helping with homework. Moreover, older fathers share homework more equally than younger ones.

To evaluate what individual characteristics matter the most in parents' division of childcare, we present in Table 6.11 the results from a set of multivariate models where the dependent variables are, respectively, the division of physical care,

6.3 Childcare and Adult Care

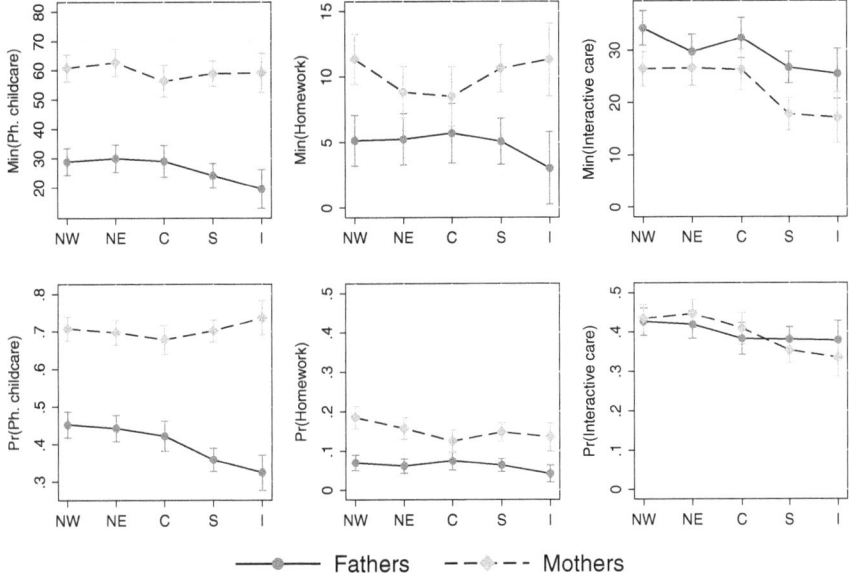

NW=North West, NE=North East, C=Centre, S=South, I=Islands

Fig. 6.3 Predicted minutes spent on and participation in three subcomponents of childcare by area of residence and gender. Mothers and fathers aged 20–64 whose children are 14 or younger. ISTAT TUS 2013–2014. Own calculations

homework and interactive care for fathers and mothers. As can be seen, most of the predictors are unrelated to the outcome. Indeed, parents' and children's age as well as marital status and partners' level of education have little if any effect on the division of care activities among parents. Non-employed mothers do more childcare

Table 6.10 Percentage contribution to childcare between parents. Mothers and fathers aged 20–64 whose children are 14 or younger. ISTAT TUS 2013–2014. Unweighted values. Own calculations

		Ph. childcare	Homework	Interactive care
		Fathers		
20–34	%	18.64	18.79	54.43
	N	355	31	281
35–44	%	24	23.59	49.84
	N	1233	284	915
45–64	%	22.65	25.46	49.90
	N	848	324	553
		Mothers		
20–34	%	77.98	83.34	44.95
	N	694	76	522
35–44	%	76.90	73.47	50.38
	N	1319	374	973
45–64	%	77.18	77.02	54.80
	N	423	189	254

in relative terms than employed ones, and having a non-employed partner significantly reduces fathers' share of childcare. Geographical area of residence follows the expected pattern: in relative terms, fathers in the South and Islands do less physical childcare and mothers more, whereas no clear pattern emerges for other types of care. Relative earned income does not systematically account for the division of childcare, whereas fathers do relatively less and mothers relatively more

Table 6.11 Multiple generalized linear models for childcare division. Fathers and mothers aged 20–64 whose children are 14 or younger. ISTAT TUS 2013–2014. Unweighted values. Own calculations

	Fathers			Mothers		
	Ph. care	Homework	Interactive care	Ph. care	Homework	Interactive care
Age class (r.c. 20–34)						
35–44	0.175	0.111	−0.057	0.208	−0.431	0.137
	(0.161)	(0.511)	(0.145)	(0.129)	(0.359)	(0.124)
45–64	0.036	0.219	0.129	0.304	−0.164	0.162
	(0.186)	(0.520)	(0.171)	(0.186)	(0.405)	(0.190)
Age of the youngest child (r.c. 0–2)						
3–5	0.155	−0.426	−0.153	−0.207	0.503	0.113
	(0.133)	(0.413)	(0.124)	(0.134)	(0.417)	(0.125)
6–10	0.072	−0.121	−0.214	−0.166	0.121	0.102
	(0.140)	(0.367)	(0.137)	(0.143)	(0.376)	(0.141)
11–14	0.260	−0.338	−0.688***	−0.366+	0.268	0.517**
	(0.183)	(0.416)	(0.191)	(0.190)	(0.429)	(0.199)
N° children	0.031	−0.024	−0.156*	−0.058	0.013	0.127+
	(0.069)	(0.141)	(0.069)	(0.069)	(0.143)	(0.070)
Not married (r.c. married)	−0.123	−0.372	0.048	0.133	0.374	−0.058
	(0.153)	(0.426)	(0.143)	(0.153)	(0.422)	(0.143)
Level of education (r.c. low ed.)						
Medium ed.	0.186	0.505*	−0.013	0.001	0.208	0.087
	(0.122)	(0.237)	(0.118)	(0.133)	(0.251)	(0.128)
High ed.	0.274+	0.352	−0.035	0.045	0.097	0.141
	(0.166)	(0.329)	(0.165)	(0.170)	(0.330)	(0.165)
Partner's level of education (r.c. low ed.)						
Medium ed.	−0.020	−0.152	−0.110	−0.189	−0.518*	0.017
	(0.133)	(0.249)	(0.128)	(0.122)	(0.238)	(0.118)
High ed.	−0.081	−0.042	−0.166	−0.295+	−0.317	0.021
	(0.169)	(0.330)	(0.164)	(0.166)	(0.329)	(0.164)
Not employed (r.c. employed)	0.170	−0.093	0.269	0.664***	0.422+	0.289*
	(0.192)	(0.371)	(0.191)	(0.124)	(0.239)	(0.120)
Partner not employed (r.c. employed)	−0.665***	−0.478+	−0.274*	−0.155	0.331	−0.243
	(0.123)	(0.244)	(0.118)	(0.191)	(0.375)	(0.188)

(continued)

6.3 Childcare and Adult Care

Table 6.11 (continued)

	Fathers			Mothers		
	Ph. care	Homework	Interactive care	Ph. care	Homework	Interactive care
Geographical area (r.c. north west)						
North east	−0.029	−0.010	−0.045	0.015	0.005	0.054
	(0.140)	(0.286)	(0.141)	(0.140)	(0.284)	(0.141)
Centre	−0.008	0.499$^+$	−0.043	−0.001	−0.506$^+$	0.057
	(0.154)	(0.297)	(0.156)	(0.154)	(0.297)	(0.156)
South	−0.283*	0.255	0.188	0.291*	−0.226	−0.176
	(0.144)	(0.270)	(0.141)	(0.144)	(0.269)	(0.141)
Islands	−0.380*	−0.222	0.194	0.374$^+$	0.209	−0.193
	(0.193)	(0.415)	(0.186)	(0.193)	(0.415)	(0.187)
Relative income (r.c. same income)						
Income > partner	−0.020	−0.472$^+$	−0.051	−0.051	0.094	0.068
	(0.126)	(0.249)	(0.128)	(0.181)	(0.363)	(0.187)
Income < partner	0.180	−0.922*	−0.137	0.156	0.429$^+$	0.048
	(0.177)	(0.395)	(0.183)	(0.125)	(0.252)	(0.130)
Week day (r.c. weekend)	−0.362***	−0.285	−0.289**	0.347**	0.273	0.286**
	(0.106)	(0.198)	(0.102)	(0.106)	(0.197)	(0.102)
Constant	−1.097***	−0.645	0.736**	0.854***	0.877	−0.726**
	(0.246)	(0.732)	(0.237)	(0.230)	(0.616)	(0.229)
N	2436	639	1749	2436	639	1749
Significance	0.000	0.000	0.000	0.000	0.000	0.000

Note r.c. = reference category. $^+p < 0.10$, $*p < 0.05$, $**p < 0.01$, $***p < 0.001$

childcare on weekdays than on weekends. This finding likely reflects institutionalized time in the Italian society that sees fathers engaged in paid work for rather long hours during the week.

We conclude this chapter with some considerations about adult care among parents. As noted, diary data is not the most apt to capture this activity. Parents in our sample who engage in adult care are few: only about 2.2% of fathers and 3.9% of mothers did any adult care on the diary day. Those who did engage, though, did so for a considerable amount of time. Interestingly, fathers in this group logged more time than mothers (45 vs. 33 min/day). Two explanations can be sought for such result. On the one hand, fathers in the sample tend to be somewhat older, and therefore are more likely to have an elder parent to tend to. Indeed, previous research suggests that kin relationships tend to trump gender when it comes to care activities (Henz 2009, 2010). On the other hand, mothers might have less time to spend caring for elder family members as they are overwhelmed with housework and childcare responsibilities. Whatever the case, the actual number of parents who engage in elder care is so low to suggest that it is definitely not a common activity among respondents in this age group.

6.4 Conclusions

This chapter illustrated gender gaps in housework, childcare and adult care during the life course stage where largest inequalities were expected: parenthood of young children. Previous studies have shown that becoming a parent has a very strong impact on women's and men's lives, and that couples shift into a traditional division of labour at the birth of a child, with women becoming more engaged in housework and childcare and men in paid work (Evertsson and Boye 2016; Schober 2013). The data presented in this chapter cannot fully test this mechanism. However, the enormous gender gap in housework among parents vs. childless women and men suggests that having a child changes time on and participation in domestic work.

When looking generally at housework participation, nearly 100% of mothers engaged in this activity on the diary day versus 70% of fathers. Above this, mothers do approximately three times the amount of housework fathers do. Gender differences appear even more acute when we look at the subcomponents of housework. Among female-typed activities, the one where fathers are more active is cooking, whereas they fall back when it comes to activities such as cleaning the house and doing the laundry. Not surprisingly, they are more likely to engage in odd jobs which are arguably more enjoyable and less time-inflexible. Still, mothers are also quite likely to engage in these tasks.

The results from the analyses revealed that the children's and the parents' age matter for the allocation of time to housework. With these data it is not possible to fully disentangle whether it is older children who require doing more housework, or whether it is older cohorts of parents who have higher standards for domestic chores and thus spend more time doing them. Whatever the case, the data show that the older the children, the wider the gender gap, and that over time mothers take up more housework of all types and fathers do not. The multivariate regressions also revealed that socio-economic factors are important predictors of housework: as shown for the childless group, higher educated and employed mothers spend less time on chores than lower educated and unemployed ones. In contrast, higher education has positive effects on fathers. Moreover, more chores are being done by women than men in the Southern area, reflecting previous findings regarding the large cultural differences that characterize the country (Dotti Sani 2012; Romano et al. 2012).

The findings for relative time on housework mirror those for absolute time quite closely, with education, employment status and geographical area of residence being the strongest predictors of the division of housework among parents. However, the results also showed that even among couples who have a rather egalitarian division of paid work or where mothers are the main earners, the division of domestic labour is far from equal.

The chapter also investigated childcare time. The results indicated that mothers' time is more than twice fathers' time and that their participation is also greater. Parents of older children spend less time on physical and interactive care than

6.4 Conclusions

parents of younger ones. This effect is especially evident among mothers. Looking at the socio-economic characteristics affecting childcare time, we find that education—along with employment status among mothers—remains a strong predictor of childcare time and participation. Indeed, highly educated mothers and fathers spend more time and engage more often in all types of childcare (Dotti Sani and Treas 2016; Guryan et al. 2008).

Finally, as for parents' time on adult care, the chapter has shown that only few parents engaged in this activity on the diary day. This result is not surprising given the sporadic nature of adult caregiving. However, the findings suggest that time use data is not the best tool to gauge time on adult care.

To conclude, the chapter showed that the allocation of time to housework among parents is very far from being gender equal when young children are present. To the contrary, this is likely the stage of the life course when the largest gaps in housework occur. In this respect, there is ample room for policy interventions to attempt to equalize parents' domestic workload. In particular, policies granting paternity leaves could encourage fathers to be more active in the domestic field, whereas more comprehensive childcare coverage could give mothers greater chances of employment and thus favour a more egalitarian division of paid and unpaid labour. Furthermore, greater employment opportunities addressed to women and mothers could significantly help to change the existing pattern of gender inequalities. As discussed in the introductory chapter, Italy lags considerably behind in international comparison in this respect, leaving ample room for improvement.

In the following chapter we address time on and participation in the domestic setting when the constraints posed by having young children should be lessened, that is among parents who are 45 or older and whose children are 15 or older. To further deepen the discussion, we shall also focus on couples in the same age group who are childless or whose children have moved out.

References

Batalova, J. A., & Cohen, P. N. (2002). Premarital cohabitation and housework: Couples in cross-national perspective. *Journal of Marriage and Family, 64*(3), 743–755.

Baxter, J., Buchler, S., Perales, F., & Western, M. (2015). A life-changing event: First births and men's and women's attitudes to mothering and gender divisions of labor. *Social Forces, 93*(3), 989–1014.

Baxter, J., Hewitt, B., & Haynes, M. (2008). Life course transitions and housework: Marriage, parenthood, and time on housework. *Journal of Marriage and Family, 70*(2), 259–272.

Bianchi, S., Lesnard, L., Nazio, T., & Raley, S. (2014). Gender and time allocation of cohabiting and married women and men in France, Italy, and the United States. *Demographic Research, 31*(8), 183–216.

Billari, F. (2004). Becoming an adult in Europe: A macro (/micro)-demographic perspective. *Demographic Research, 3*, 15–44.

Blood, R., & Wolfe, D. (1960). *Husbands and wives: The dynamics of married living*. New York, NY: Free Press.

Brayfield, A. A. (1992). Employment resources and housework in Canada. *Journal of Marriage and the Family, 54*(1), 19–30.

Brines, J. (1994). Economic dependency, gender, and the division of labor at home. *American Journal of Sociology, 100*(3), 652–688.

Dotti Sani, G. M. (2012). La divisione del lavoro domestico e delle attività di cura nelle coppie italiane: un'analisi empirica. *Stato e Mercato., 94*(1), 161–192.

Dotti Sani, G. M., & Treas, J. (2016). Educational gradients in parents' child-care time across countries, 1965–2012. *Journal of Marriage and Family, 78*(4), 1083–1096.

England, P., & Srivastava, A. (2013). Educational differences in US parents' time spent in child care: The role of culture and cross-spouse influence. *Social Science Research, 42*(4), 971–988.

Evertsson, M., & Boye, K. (2016). The gendered transition to parenthood: Lasting inequalities in the home and in the labor market. In Emerging trends in the social and behavioral sciences: An interdisciplinary, searchable, and linkable resource. Published Online: 29/11/2016.

Ferree, M. M. (1990). Beyond separate spheres: Feminism and family research. *Journal of Marriage and the Family, 50*(4), 866–884.

Gough, M., & Killewald, A. (2011). Unemployment in families: The case of housework. *Journal of Marriage and Family, 73*(5), 1085–1100.

Grunow, D., & Evertsson, M. (2016). *Couples' Transitions to Parenthood*. Cheltenham, UK Northampton, MA, USA: Edward Elgar.

Guryan, J., Hurst, E., & Kearney, M. (2008). Parental education and parental time with children. *The Journal of Economic Perspectives, 22*(3), 23–46.

Hays, S. (1996). *The cultural contradictions of motherhood*. New Haven, CT: Yale University Press.

Henz, U. (2009). Couples' provision of informal care for parents and parents-in-law: Far from sharing equally? *Ageing & Society, 29*(03), 369–395.

Henz, U. (2010). Parent care as unpaid family labor: How do spouses share? *Journal of Marriage and Family, 72*(1), 148–164.

Hiller, D. V. (1984). Power dependence and division of family work. *Sex Roles, 10*(11–12), 1003–1019.

Hoekzema, E., Barba-Müller, E., Pozzobon, C., Picado, M., et al. (2017). Pregnancy leads to long-lasting changes in human brain structure. *Nature Neuroscience, 20*, 287–296.

Katz-Wise, S. L., Priess, H. A., & Hyde, J. S. (2010). Gender-role attitudes and behavior across the transition to parenthood. *Developmental Psychology, 46*(1), 18–28.

Lareau, A. (2000). Social class and the daily lives of children. A study from the United States. *Childhood, 7*(2), 155–171.

Romano, M. C., Mencarini, L., & Tanturri, M. L. (2012). *Uso del tempo e ruoli di genere Tra lavoro e famiglia nel ciclo di vita*. Rome: Istituto Nazionale di Statistica.

Sayer, L. C., Gauthier, A. H., & Furstenberg, F. F. (2004). Educational differences in parents' time with children: Cross-national variations. *Journal of Marriage and Family, 66*(5), 1152–1169.

Schober, P. S. (2013). The parenthood effect on gender inequality: Explaining the change in paid and domestic work when British couples become parents. *European Sociological Review, 29*(1), 74–85.

Sullivan, O., Billari, F. C., & Altintas, E. (2014). Fathers' changing contributions to child care and domestic work in very low-fertility countries the effect of education. *Journal of Family Issues, 35*(8), 1048–1065.

Szinovacz, M. E. (2000). Changes in housework after retirement: A panel analysis. *Journal of Marriage and Family, 62*(1), 78–92.

Chapter 7
When the Kids Grow up: Domestic Work Among Italians Aged 45–64

Abstract In this chapter, the focus shifts to parents of children aged 15 and above. It also includes a comparison with childless Italians between 45 and 64 years old. The chapter illustrates that at this stage, like the previous ones, gender and household status have a large impact on housework. Coupled women perform more housework than single ones, with differences being greater when children are present. The pattern for participation in housework is similar, but with an evident ceiling effect for women. Education is once again a crucial element for housework time, with highly educated women spending less time on chores than lower educated ones. Not being employed and living in the Southern area of the country are also associated with doing more housework for women. For men, education has no effect on housework while non-employed men do more housework than employed ones. Finally, as for other age groups, Southern men spend less time on housework compared to those in other regions. The chapter also illustrates how relatively little time is spent caring for other adults among subjects in this age group.

Keywords Domestic work · Housework · Adult care · Children
Gender differences · Fathers · Mothers · Motherhood · Fatherhood
Aging · Life course · Italy · Italian Time Use Survey

7.1 Introduction

This chapter has the aim of exploring housework and other forms of domestic work among Italians who are at a mature age, that is, between 45 and 64 years old. This is an interesting phase to focus on because the requirements from the domestic sphere should be less demanding compared to other stages, such as when young children are present (Baxter et al. 2008). At the same time, ulterior care needs may emerge from other aging family members. Since these typically fall on women's shoulders more than on men's, new scenarios for gender inequalities may appear (Henz 2009). Therefore, this chapter focuses on gender inequalities in housework and care activities among mature couples. Beyond descriptive accounts of time on and participation in domestic work, it explores the relation between individual resources and constraints—in terms of education and employment status—and time on housework, degree of participation in it, and share of domestic work done by partners (Blood and Wolfe 1960; Brines 1994). The chapter also offers a three-way comparison among different types of couples: parents of children aged 15 and above, couples whose children have moved out, and childless couples. This allows us to tease out important differences in the way couples manage domestic work while keeping into account varying configurations of time and power as well as "rooted habits" that might have emerged in earlier years. Thus, unlike most studies that focus on adults generally or only on parents, the focus on childless couples offers a more comprehensive view of the problem under consideration. Moreover, the chapter also offers a brief comparison between couples and single women and men, to further explore differences tied to parenthood status, gender and age.

7.2 Housework Time Among Mature Couples: Growing Differences Between Women and Men?

Before moving to the sample of mature couples central to this chapter, we briefly dwell on a comparison between couples and singles. Figure 7.1 shows average minutes of general housework on the diary day as well as the percentages of individuals who engaged in this activity. The plot is subset by gender and by life course stage, differentiating between childless singles, singles whose children have moved out, childless couples, couples whose children have moved out, and couples with co-resident children (i.e. parents). The figure illustrates the effects of life course events on women's and men's housework time and participation, showing that there are very large differences in housework time between childless women and mothers of co-resident children. Single childless women do about 3 h and a half of housework on the diary day, while coupled women with co-resident children do 5 h and 40 min. In contrast, the differences between the two "extreme" groups of men are much smaller: 130 versus 118 min. Differences in participation among women are more moderate, but there is evidence of a ceiling effect as nearly 100% of women engage in some housework on the diary day. Differences among men are larger, as singles engage more in domestic work than coupled men. This points once again to moderate specialization effects over the life course. These preliminary figures indicate that the housework load for women becomes larger over the life course, whereas for men it tends to reduce. In the following paragraphs, we limit the attention to couples as they represent the majority of individuals in this age group.

Table 7.1 reports summary statistics for the sample of couples considered in this chapter. We focus on adult couples between 45 and 64 years who are either childless, whose children have left the parental home, or whose children still live at home and are 15 or older. Beyond predictable values of age and age of the children, most couples are married, with parents being the most likely to have formalized

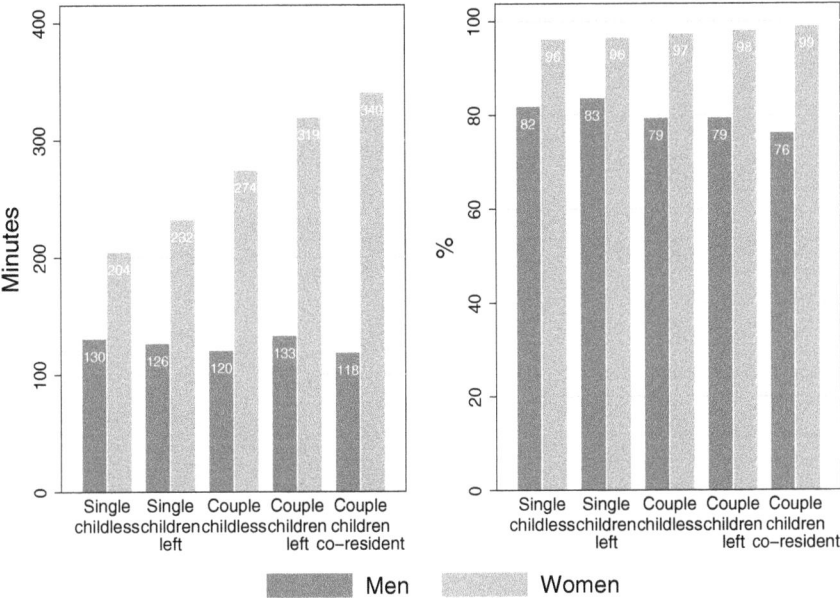

Fig. 7.1 Average minutes spent on (right) and average participation in (left) housework. Women and men aged 45–64. ISTAT TUS 2013–2014. Unweighted values. Own calculations

their union and childless couples the least. Interesting findings emerge for education, with childless women being by large the most highly educated, thus suggesting issues of selection and tempo effects when it comes to fertility choices (Ní Bhrolcháin and Beaujouan 2012). Indeed, studies have shown that childlessness is more common among higher educated women and, less so, men. While our data are not set up to validate this expectation, we can notice that the childless women in the sample tend to be better educated than mothers (18% vs. 13%). As far as employment status is concerned, parents of resident children and childless men are more likely to be employed than parents of children who have left, likely due to age differences. Over 70% of childless men and fathers of co-resident children are employed against 50% of those whose children have moved out. Similarly, among mothers whose children have left the parental home, only 34% are employed against 50% among the other two groups. As for relative income contributions, the data show that the most egalitarian couples are the childless ones: about 35% of these couples are likely to contribute about the same amount versus 28% of parents whose children have moved out and 26% of parents of co-resident children. In contrast, parents of co-resident children are more likely to have a traditional male-breadwinning arrangement. We shall look more in detail at the effects of these individual and household characteristics in the multivariate analyses that follow.

Moving now to a descriptive analysis of the various subcomponents of domestic work, Table 7.2 reports average minutes and percentages of participation in domestic activities by gender and age group. Starting from general housework, we

Table 7.1 Summary statistics by life stage and gender. Coupled men and women aged 45–64. ISTAT TUS 2013–2014. Unweighted values. Own calculations

	Men			Women		
	Childless	Children moved out	Parent	Childless	Children moved out	Parent
Age of youngest child %						
15–19			37			31
20–24			34			33
25–29			20			22
30–34			7			10
≥ 35			2			4
Number of children (mean)	0	0	1.6	0	0	1.6
Marital status %						
Married	85	94	98	86	96	98
Not married	15	6	2	14	4	2
Level of education %						
Low	45	59	50	44	63	50
Medium	44	33	37	38	29	37
High	11	8	13	18	7	13
Employment status %						
Employed	72	51	75	51	34	51
Not employed	28	49	25	49	66	49
Geographical area %						
North West	30	22	19	32	21	19
North east	23	23	19	21	24	19
Centre	18	21	17	17	19	17
South	20	24	34	21	26	33
Islands	9	11	11	9	10	12
Division of household income %						
Respondent more	50	61	64	13	11	8
About the same	35	28	26	34	28	27
Respondent less	15	11	10	53	61	64
Day of the week %						
Weekend	67	65	66	69	65	65
Weekday	33	35	34	31	35	35
N	398	641	2136	429	1004	3761

can observe that men perform similar amounts regardless of life course stage. Participation is also quite similar. Mothers of co-resident children, instead, spend much more time on housework than mothers of children who have moved out and childless women. This suggests not only that most of the extra work stemming from children's presence falls on women's shoulders, but also that behavioural patterns that are acquired when children are present do not disappear completely. In contrast, participation in chores is nearly 100% for all women in this age group. Looking at the subcomponents of housework, we can recognize patterns already highlighted in previous chapters. Of all activities, men are most likely to engage in cooking (∼48% across age groups) and odd jobs (∼60% across age groups). Only in the latter, however, do they spend considerable amounts of time. About 90% of women engage in cooking and cleaning activities on the diary day and they do so for ∼130 and ∼100 min respectively. Generally speaking, mothers of co-resident children spend more time on all chores and engage more frequently in them compared to childless women. The largest life course difference among women concerns cooking, as mothers do ∼140 min/day and ∼135 min/day respectively for those with co-resident children or whose children have left. Childless women, in contrast spend about 110 min per day cooking. These descriptive statistics suggest that gender and stage of the life course are relevant predictors of housework time among mature women and men.

In the multivariate regressions presented in Table 7.3, we can see the association between housework time and relevant individual and household characteristics. Confirming the results from the descriptive statistics, the models indicate that

Table 7.2 Average minutes spent on and average participation in domestic work. Coupled women and men aged 45–64. ISTAT TUS 2013–2014. Unweighted values. Own calculations

	Men		Women	
	Min.	%	Min.	%
Housework				
Childless	119	79	273	97
Children left	133	79	319	98
Parents	118	76	340	99
Cooking				
Childless	29	53	110	93
Children left	25	48	135	94
Parents	23	45	140	96
Cleaning				
Childless	23	37	86	83
Children left	23	35	102	89
Parents	20	30	107	90
Washing				
Childless	0.48	1.5	30	38
Children left	0.55	2.2	32	42
Parents	0.65	1.8	39	49
Odd jobs				
Childless	66	53	48	56
Children left	84	64	50	58
Parents	74	60	54	62

Table 7.3 Multiple regression models. Dependent variables: daily minutes spent cooking, cleaning and washing, and doing odd jobs. Coupled women and men aged 45–64. ISTAT TUS 2013–2014. Unweighted values. Own calculations

	Women			Men		
	Cook	Clean and wash	Odd jobs	Cook	Clean and wash	Odd jobs
Life stage (r.c. couple childless)						
Couple child out	12.661**	6.872	0.454	−4.897	−0.716	7.574
	(4.497)	(5.715)	(3.951)	(2.705)	(3.063)	(6.684)
Parent	24.684***	24.753***	6.778	−2.741	−0.341	9.161
	(4.128)	(5.247)	(3.627)	(2.336)	(2.646)	(5.773)
Not married (r.c. married)	−7.813	2.457	0.347	−4.641	3.535	2.869
	(6.628)	(8.424)	(5.823)	(3.655)	(4.139)	(9.033)
Level of education (r.c. low ed.)						
Medium ed.	−15.307***	−9.404**	2.826	4.761**	1.780	−4.911
	(2.842)	(3.612)	(2.497)	(1.621)	(1.836)	(4.007)
High ed.	−20.516***	−29.431***	7.140	6.219*	−2.879	−5.436
	(4.199)	(5.337)	(3.689)	(2.448)	(2.772)	(6.049)
Not employed (r.c. employed)	40.905***	34.457***	15.631***	12.629***	11.440***	46.787***
	(2.903)	(3.689)	(2.550)	(1.701)	(1.926)	(4.203)
Geographical area (r.c. north west)						
North east	−8.258*	−7.213	−6.202	−1.211	−1.506	−0.927
	(3.881)	(4.932)	(3.409)	(2.296)	(2.600)	(5.675)
Centre	8.106*	1.138	−4.277	−4.691*	−6.137*	4.545
	(4.045)	(5.141)	(3.553)	(2.379)	(2.695)	(5.880)
South	17.416***	17.118***	−8.674**	−11.369***	−9.549***	1.227
	(3.605)	(4.582)	(3.167)	(2.116)	(2.396)	(5.229)
						(continued)

Table 7.3 (continued)

	Women			Men		
	Cook	Clean and wash	Odd jobs	Cook	Clean and wash	Odd jobs
Islands	17.251***	34.688***	−9.723*	−1.324	−5.448	10.301
	(4.684)	(5.952)	(4.114)	(2.780)	(3.148)	(6.870)
Relative income (r.c. same income)						
Income > partner	1.031	3.803	−1.080	−6.182***	−3.650	2.421
	(4.657)	(5.919)	(4.091)	(1.710)	(1.936)	(4.226)
Income < partner	13.193***	9.381*	3.006	5.656*	4.101	10.518
	(3.013)	(3.829)	(2.647)	(2.675)	(3.029)	(6.610)
Week day (r.c. weekend)	−5.308*	1.213	3.020	−2.648	−5.973***	−16.184***
	(2.631)	(3.344)	(2.312)	(1.557)	(1.763)	(3.847)
Constant	89.840***	96.049***	40.138***	29.804***	26.533***	56.342***
	(5.235)	(6.653)	(4.599)	(2.965)	(3.358)	(7.328)
N	3761	3761	3761	3175	3175	3175
Significance	0.000	0.000	0.000	0.000	0.000	0.000

Note r.c. = reference category. *$p < 0.05$, **$p < 0.01$, ***$p < 0.001$

mothers with co-resident children spend nearly 25 min more cooking and cleaning and washing the house compared to childless mothers. Mothers whose children have moved out also do more of the considered activities but the differences are not always statistically significant. The results for men indicate no life stage differences whatsoever: regardless of parental status, men between 45 and 64 spend roughly the same amount of time on chores. Education proves once again to be a strong predictor of time on housework: medium and high educated women spend considerably less time cooking and cleaning than low educated ones. Highly educated women do especially less cleaning and washing than low educated ones (29 min less per day). Men's education, in contrast, is statistically significant only for cooking time, with medium and high educated men spending a little more time on this activity compared to low educated ones. Employment status has a rather strong effect for both genders: women and men who are not employed spend significantly more time on all three activities compared to employed ones. The largest difference among women is in cooking time (113 vs. 154 min/day), whereas among men it is in time on odd jobs (60 vs. 107 min/day). It is remarkable that the largest difference emerges for the activities that are considered the most pleasurable, as to indicate that non-employed women and men can decide to spend their extra time on things they enjoy rather than others. It is also interesting to note that these are gender-specific: cooking for women and odd jobs for men. The findings for geographical area point once again to the greater time investments made by women in the South (17 extra minutes per day spent cooking and cleaning and washing) and Islands (17 extra minutes per day more cooking and 34 min washing and cleaning). Conversely, men in the South spend 11 and 9 min less cooking and washing and cleaning respectively. Finally, we can observe that women and men who earn less than their partners contribute something more to all activities, but the results are only significant for cooking and washing and cleaning among women and only for cooking among men. These findings are in line with resource theory but are not always found in empirical studies.

In Table 7.4 we move to another relevant aspect: the division of domestic chores among couples. Childless men and women and parents whose children have left the home are those who share chores more equally, but they are still very far from equality. Fathers in these two groups do about 28% of general housework versus 23% among fathers of co-resident children. The picture changes if we look at the sub-components of housework: men contribute considerably less to cooking and cleaning and washing than they do to odd jobs. For example, childless men do 21% of the cooking and only 16% of the washing and cleaning. Fathers of co-resident children do even less: 14% of the cooking and 11% of the washing and cleaning. These values indicate that the division of overall housework is strongly driven by men's contribution to odd jobs, which, as discussed, do not form the bulk of routine and mostly unpleasant domestic work.

How do individual and household characteristics affect the division of chores between partners? Table 7.5 reports the results for the multivariate generalized linear models where the dependent variable represents the share of housework performed by each partner (0 stands for the respondent doing none of the housework and 1 for

Table 7.4 Average division of domestic chores by gender and life course stage (%). Coupled men and women aged 45–64. ISTAT TUS 2013–2014. Unweighted values. Own calculations

	Housework	Cooking	Cleaning and washing	Odd jobs
Men				
Childless	28.26	21.05	16.84	49.89
N	396	384	360	298
Children left	28.03	16.44	13.91	58.07
N	637	620	597	508
Parents	23.64	14.26	11.20	51.74
N	2124	2090	2000	1714
Women				
Childless	71.18	79.66	82.95	45.99
N	425	413	388	322
Children left	71.83	84.13	85.56	40.56
N	996	977	941	801
Parents	76.14	85.88	88.76	47.35
N	2313	2277	2185	1882

doing all the housework). The results are similar to those for absolute time but there are some important differences. First, we can notice that fathers of co-resident children do less cooking and cleaning and washing than childless fathers. The effects, however, are small and not statistically significant. Instead, mothers with co-resident children do more cooking and washing and cleaning than other women, but not more odd jobs. Marital status does not affect the division of chores (except for unmarried women who share odd jobs more evenly) and neither does the level of education. In contrast, individuals who are not employed are likely to undertake a greater share of chores than employed ones. Specifically, employed women do 82% of the cooking while the non-employed do 88%. Similar differences emerge for washing and cleaning (85% vs. 90%). Conversely, non-employed men do 18% of the cooking and employed ones 13%. The difference for washing and cleaning is also about 5 percentage points (15% vs. 10%), whereas the gap for odd jobs is much larger: non-employed men do 66% of this activity and employed ones 46%. These results fall in line with time availability theories (Blood and Wolfe 1960; Brines 1994). To account for relative resources, the models also include the partner's level of education. Having a highly educated partner has a positive effect on men's share of cooking, while the coefficients for the other activities are positive but not significant. Among women, instead, the partner's education has no statistically significant effect on any of the three activities. Once again, women in the South contribute considerably more to typically female chores in relative terms than in other regions, and men less. For example, men do about 19% of the cooking in the North-West and about 9% in the South. Conversely, women do 85% of the washing and cleaning in the North-West and 91% in the South. The results for relative income are also quite interesting. In line with relative resource theory, both women and men who out-earn their partner

Table 7.5 Multiple generalized linear models. Dependent variable: partners' share of cooking, cleaning and washing, and doing odd jobs. Coupled men and women aged 45–64. ISTAT TUS 2013–2014. Un weighted values. Own calculations

	Men			Women		
	Cook	Clean and wash	Odd jobs	Cook	Clean and wash	Odd jobs
Life stage (r.c. couples childless)						
Couples child-out	−0.214	−0.190	0.220	0.073	0.027	−0.218
	(0.173)	(0.193)	(0.156)	(0.158)	(0.171)	(0.139)
Parents	−0.266[+]	−0.259	0.153	0.313*	0.350*	0.059
	(0.148)	(0.166)	(0.134)	(0.144)	(0.159)	(0.127)
Not married (r.c. married)	0.025	0.086	−0.223	0.030	−0.019	0.446*
	(0.240)	(0.261)	(0.211)	(0.236)	(0.251)	(0.204)
Level of education (r.c. low ed.)						
Medium ed.	0.086	0.073	−0.019	−0.209[+]	0.007	0.079
	(0.126)	(0.140)	(0.103)	(0.120)	(0.132)	(0.096)
High ed.	0.248	0.028	−0.060	−0.254	−0.220	0.113
	(0.191)	(0.225)	(0.162)	(0.177)	(0.194)	(0.152)
Not employed (r.c. employed)	0.376***	0.495***	0.840***	0.525***	0.385**	0.146[+]
	(0.114)	(0.125)	(0.096)	(0.109)	(0.119)	(0.087)
Partner's level of education (r.c. low ed.)						
Medium ed.	0.357**	0.137	0.041	−0.092	−0.018	0.116
	(0.126)	(0.140)	(0.103)	(0.117)	(0.128)	(0.094)
High ed.	0.497**	0.330	0.151	−0.241	−0.012	0.224
	(0.186)	(0.210)	(0.163)	(0.176)	(0.201)	(0.149)

(continued)

7.2 Housework Time Among Mature Couples: Growing Differences …

Table 7.5 (continued)

	Men			Women		
	Cook	Clean and wash	Odd jobs	Cook	Clean and wash	Odd jobs
Geographical area (r.c. north west)						
North east	0.069	0.172	0.116	-0.012	-0.083	-0.136
	(0.144)	(0.157)	(0.130)	(0.134)	(0.144)	(0.116)
Centre	-0.198	-0.275	0.045	0.153	0.175	-0.097
	(0.155)	(0.176)	(0.133)	(0.145)	(0.159)	(0.122)
South	-0.708***	-0.707***	0.066	0.599***	0.639***	-0.109
	(0.152)	(0.169)	(0.119)	(0.140)	(0.153)	(0.109)
Islands	-0.168	-0.435*	0.221	0.084	0.357⁺	-0.300*
	(0.185)	(0.215)	(0.157)	(0.171)	(0.194)	(0.140)
Relative income (r.c. same income)						
Income > partner	-0.429***	-0.357**	-0.281**	-0.394**	-0.373*	-0.108
	(0.115)	(0.130)	(0.098)	(0.148)	(0.165)	(0.143)
Income < partner	0.161	0.158	0.139	0.327**	0.224⁺	0.317***
	(0.161)	(0.179)	(0.153)	(0.110)	(0.121)	(0.092)
Week day (r.c. weekend)	0.015	-0.095	-0.681***	-0.078	-0.054	0.564***
	(0.107)	(0.121)	(0.087)	(0.098)	(0.108)	(0.078)
Constant	-1.446***	-1.602***	0.024	1.134***	1.273***	-0.656***
	(0.196)	(0.219)	(0.175)	(0.184)	(0.201)	(0.162)
N	3094	2957	2520	3667	3514	3005
Significance	0.000	0.000	0.000	0.000	0.000	0.000

Note r.c. = reference category. ⁺$p < 0.10$, *$p < 0.05$, **$p < 0.01$, ***$p < 0.001$

do less chores. For instance, men and women who earn more than their partner do, respectively, 12% and 77% of the cooking, whereas the figures are 20% and 88% for subjects who contribute less to the overall household income. Similar results emerge for washing and cleaning and, for men, odd jobs.

7.3 Emerging Care Needs from Frail Family Members

Lastly, we discuss the allocation of time to adult care. In this age group we except women and men to become progressively more engaged in this activity because, on the one hand, their parents are becoming older and more in need of help and, on the other hand, some of them—mostly women—might have partners who also need care (Henz 2009, 2010; Saraceno 1994).

Table 7.6 reports time on and participation in adult care among women and men aged 45–64 in the three life course stages considered in this chapter. The results from the table indicate that adult care is performed by a minority of individuals. Considering the very small number of subjects involved in these tasks, the figures we present need to be taken *cum grano salis*, as they are subject to a certain degree of statistical uncertainty. In general, it is women who engage the most in this task in all three age groups. However, among those who do engage, men spend slightly more time than women. Looking at variations among the life course stages, parents whose children have left the parental home are those who spend more time on adult care (80 min among men and 62 min among women), followed by childless adults. Thus, although women engage in adult care in greater percentages than men, the latter engage in this activity for relatively long spans of time.

Table 7.6 Average minutes spent on and participation in adult care. Coupled men and women aged 45–64. ISTAT TUS 2013–2014. Unweighted values. Own calculations

	Men		Women	
	Mean	N	Mean	N
Childless				
Min.	1.91	398	3.85	429
%	3.52		6.53	
Min.–doers	54.29	14	58.93	28
Children left				
Min.	3.12	641	2.48	1,004
%	3.9		3.98	
Min.–doers	80	25	62.25	40
Parents				
Min.	1.72	2,136	4.41	2,328
%	3.84		10.27	
Min.–doers	44.88	82	42.93	239

7.4 Conclusions

This chapter has centred on housework and adult care among couples between 45 and 64 years old. Specifically, it has looked at parents of co-resident children aged 15 and above, parents whose children have already left the parental home and childless adults. This three-way comparison provided a broad focus on this age group while focusing on life course stage differences as well as gender differences. The chapter revealed important differences between women and men: in all three stages of the life course, women engage more often than men in general housework, cooking, cleaning and washing and odd jobs; they also spend more time on these activities than men. The chapter also confirmed previous findings by showing that childless couples are the ones who share chores more equally (Baxter et al. 2008). It is important to note, however, that childless couples display a more egalitarian allocation of time to housework not because of men's behaviour, but rather because of women's. Indeed, men's allocation of time to chores remains rather similar in the three groups considered, while mothers of co-resident children spend considerably more time on chores than childless women. The results, therefore, fall in line with previous studies showing how the presence of children, even older ones, has deep and gendered consequences for the household work load (Baxter et al. 2008; Schober 2013). The findings also confirm the importance of time availability, relative resources and cultural norms among this age group: individual level of education, employment status, area of residence and relative income all play some role in the allocation of time to housework as well as in the division of domestic chores between partners (Blood and Wolfe 1960; Brines 1994; Dotti Sani 2012).

The chapter also brought the attention to adult care. The results indicate that, in this age group, few subjects devote much time to this activity. However, as mentioned in previous chapters, the nature of the instrument used to collect the data—the time diary—likely leads to an underestimation of this activity. In general, women are more likely to engage in adult care than men, but men who engage in adult care spend considerable amounts of time on it. To summarize, our results reveal large gender differences in domestic work among mature women and men, that are exacerbated by the presence of children. In the next chapter, we shall explore the final stage of the life course—the empty nest—to evaluate gender differences in housework and adult care among women and men aged 65 and above who are childless or whose children have left the parental home.

References

Baxter, J., Hewitt, B., & Haynes, M. (2008). Life course transitions and housework: Marriage, parenthood, and time on housework. *Journal of Marriage and Family, 70*(2), 259–272.

Blood, R., & Wolfe, D. (1960). *Husbands and wives: The dynamics of married living*. New York, NY: Free Press.

Brines, J. (1994). Economic dependency, gender, and the division of labor at home. *American Journal of Sociology, 100*(3), 652–688.
Dotti Sani, G. M. (2012). La divisione del lavoro domestico e delle attività di cura nelle coppie italiane: un'analisi empirica. *Stato e Mercato, 94*(1), 161–192.
Henz, U. (2009). Couples' provision of informal care for parents and parents-in-law: Far from sharing equally? *Ageing & Society, 29*(03), 369–395.
Henz, U. (2010). Parent care as unpaid family labor: How do spouses share? *Journal of Marriage and Family, 72*(1), 148–164.
Ní Bhrolcháin, M., & Beaujouan, E. (2012). Fertility postponement is largely due to rising educational enrolment. *Population Studies, 66*(3), 311–327.
Saraceno, C. (1994). The ambivalent familism of the Italian welfare state. *Social Politics, 1*(1), 60–82.
Schober, P. S. (2013). The parenthood effect on gender inequality: Explaining the change in paid and domestic work when British couples become parents. *European Sociological Review, 29*(1), 74–85.

Chapter 8
In the Empty Nest: Housework and Adult Care Among Italians Aged 65 and Above

Abstract This chapter considers the allocation of housework time among women and men aged 65 and above. In this group, we find large differences by gender and household status, with differences between women and men being largest among couples and smallest among singles, once again pointing to the relevance of specialization even among an age group where above 90% of subjects are (no longer) employed. Despite the relatively low level of education among this group, the educational variable is still a rather strong predictor of housework time for these elder Italians. Area of residence also accounts for some of the time spent on chores by men while employment status has a significant effect for both genders. Moreover, age is an important predictor of housework time. Among the oldest of the old, gender differences in housework time virtually disappear. Average minutes on adult care as well as percentages of engaged subjects are very low, reinforcing the notion that time use data are not the best tool to study time on adult care.

Keywords Domestic work · Housework · Adult care · Gender differences
Aging · Life course · Italy · Italian time use survey

8.1 Introduction

This chapter focuses on an aspect that is often neglected in the study of the allocation of time to domestic chores, that is, housework among elder women and men. By going beyond working age individuals, the chapter provides fresh insights into the embeddedness of norms about domestic work in a context of low gender equality. The analyses also focus on time spent on and participation in adult care among elder Italians. The chapter looks at single individuals as well as subjects who are in a partnership. In both cases, we distinguish between childless individuals and parents whose children have left the parental home. Since the scope of the chapter is to explore the empty nest phase, we do not engage in a comparison with parents of co-resident children. For singles as well as for couples, we explore to what extent individual resources such as level of education and employment status affect housework. When looking at couples, we also investigate the division of domestic chores and its association with the partners' characteristics (Blood and Wolfe 1960; Brines 1994). We expect respondents—in particular women—to devote increasing amounts of time to the care of adult family members (Chesley and Poppie 2009; Henz 2009, 2010; Sarkisian and Gerstel 2004). However, individual factors such as kinship, economic resources, geographical proximity and availability of alternative care givers have been shown to play an important part in this respect (Barnett 2013; Henz 2006; Szinovacz and Davey 2008). Due to the small number of subjects who engaged in adult care on the diary day, we cannot provide a fine-grained analysis of this activity. Thus, we devote Sect. 8.4 to a descriptive yet informative account of the phenomena.

8.2 Housework Among Elder Adults

The sample analysed in this chapter comprises women and men in the later stage of their life, that is, ages 65 and above. Table 8.1 reports summary statistics for this group of individuals. Women and men whose children have left the parental home tend to be older than the rest, and virtually all couples are married. The table also shows that most subjects are lower educated, consistent with the large generational changes in levels of education in Italy over the past decades (Eurostat 2017b). Importantly, men are better educated than women, representing thus a predictable exception compared to the other age groups analysed in the volume. Similarly, the majority of the sample is not employed, as most subjects are well beyond retirement age and many of the women were probably full-time homemakers throughout the life course (Eurostat 2017a). Indeed, even in this age group, men have a slightly higher chance of being in employment.

Moving to a description of domestic work among women and men in this age group, Fig. 8.1 shows average minutes spent on general housework on the diary day as well as the percentage of those who did at least 10 min of housework on that day. The first thing to notice, when it comes to average minutes, is that the smallest gender differences can be observed among singles: regardless of parental status, women do the least and men the most housework in this group. In contrast, women do much more housework, and men considerably less, when they are in a couple. For example, single childless women do 226 min of housework per day while men in the same group 172. Mothers whose children have left, in contrast, do 327 min per day and men only 135. Once again, we find evidence of task specialization: even among elder couples whose available time should not be influenced by large differences in working status, women spend more time taking care of the home than men. Considering the high age of the sample, this likely reflects cultural norms of what behaviour is appropriate for women and men, as well as long lasting habits. The results for participation are similar, but within-gender differences are smaller. Participation ranges from 88% among single childless women to 97% among

8.2 Housework Among Elder Adults

Table 8.1 Summary statistics by life stage and gender. Men and women aged 65 and above. ISTAT TUS 2013–2014. Unweighted values. Own calculations

	Men						Women					
	Single		Couple		Single		Single		Couple		Single	
	Childless	Children left	Childless	Children left	Childless	Children left	Childless	Children left	Childless	Children left		
Age group %												
65–74	56	39	55	53	34	29	63	63				
≥75	44	61	45	47	66	71	37	37				
Marital status %												
Married			95	98			95	99				
Not married			5	2			5	1				
Level of education %												
Low	74	72	72	74	76	85	74	81				
Medium	17	18	18	18	17	11	18	15				
High	9	10	10	8	6	4	7	4				
Employment status %												
Employed	7	7	5	6	2	2	1	0.2				
Not employed	93	93	95	94	98	98	99	98				
Geographical area %												
North West	26	25	30	23	22	23	29	23				
North East	26	19	19	22	19	21	20	22				
Centre	18	18	21	19	21	20	21	20				
South	19	31	22	27	24	27	22	26				
Islands	11	7	9	8	15	9	8	8				

(continued)

Table 8.1 (continued)

	Men				Women			
	Single		Couple		Single		Couple	
	Childless	Children left	Childless	Children left	Childless	Children left	Childless	Children left
Division of household income %								
Respondent more			54	61			6	6
About the same			38	32			39	32
Respondent less			7	7			55	62
Day of the week %								
Weekend	65	70	70	66	65	66	70	67
Weekday	35	30	30	34	35	34	30	33
N	303	473	313	2096	564	1829	238	1692

8.2 Housework Among Elder Adults

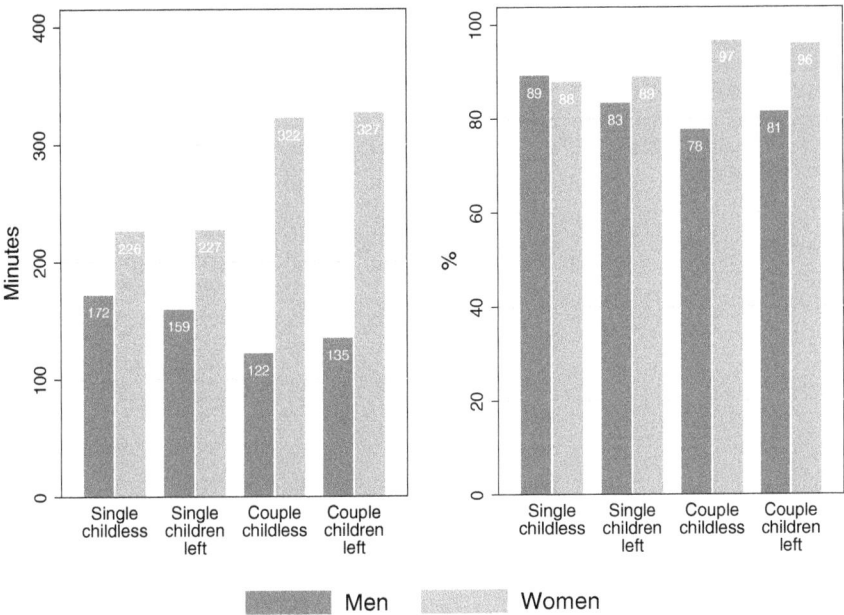

Fig. 8.1 Average minutes on (left) and average participation in (right) housework. Women and men aged 65 and above. ISTAT TUS 2013–2014. Unweighted values. Own calculations

partnered childless ones. Among men, the values are close to 80% across all four groups.

In Table 8.2 we report time on and participation in the various subcomponents of housework: cooking, cleaning the house, washing, ironing, mending clothes etc., and odd jobs. Differences tied to partnership status are visible for some of the subcomponents. For example, single men spend over one hour a day cooking, while partnered men half of that time (∼30 min). The percentages of men who engage in cooking are also much smaller among partnered ones (∼44% vs. ∼75%). Coupled women, instead, spend more time cooking than singles ones (∼145 min/day vs. 100 min/day), and they are somewhat more likely to engage in this task (∼94% vs. ∼84%). When it comes to the other activities, differences related to partnership status among men are less evident, suggesting that single men might be scaling down their effort or might be outsourcing these tasks. Differences among women are clearly visible when it comes to cleaning and washing clothes. When it comes to odd jobs, partnered men tend to do somewhat more than singles, whereas no clear pattern emerges among women.

The multivariate models presented in Table 8.3 allow us to investigate the effect of individual characteristics on the allocation of time to the various sub-components of domestic work. The coefficients reveal important pieces of information. First of all, age has a relatively strong and negative effect among women, suggesting that gender differences decline over time. We shall comment more upon this finding in

Table 8.2 Average minutes spent on and average participation in housework. Men and women aged 65 and above. ISTAT TUS 2013–2014. Unweighted values. Own calculations

	Men		Women	
	Min.	%	Min.	%
Housework				
Single, childless	172	89	226	88
Single, children left	159	83	227	89
Couple, childless	122	78	322	97
Couple, children left	135	81	327	96
Cooking				
Single, childless	71	79	97	84
Single, children left	64	73	103	85
Couple, childless	29	44	146	93
Couple, children left	29	45	149	94
Cleaning				
Single, childless	34	53	70	71
Single, children left	36	51	66	74
Couple, childless	19	31	97	87
Couple, children left	23	34	101	88
Washing				
Single, childless	1.9	5.3	17	24
Single, children left	2.2	5.3	22	28
Couple, childless	0.16	0.64	29	38
Couple, children left	0.67	1.7	34	42
Odd jobs				
Single, childless	65	62	42	51
Single, children left	58	59	36	48
Couple, childless	74	64	50	58
Couple, children left	82	67	43	54

the conclusions of the chapter. The coefficients for the life course stage confirm the large differences that emerged from the descriptive statistics when it comes to cooking, cleaning and washing, but not odd jobs for women, and mostly for cooking for men. Similar to other age groups, level of education and employment status affect the various components of housework time, with better educated women and all employed subjects spending less time on domestic work. For example, highly educated women do nearly half an hour less of cooking on the diary day, 15 min less of cleaning and washing, and 15 extra minutes of odd jobs compared to low educated ones. The coefficients for education are not significant among men except for odd jobs (−17 min/day). As emerged in previous analyses, non-employed women and men spend more time on housework but the type of activity matters a lot. Indeed, non-employed women spend considerable extra time cooking and men doing odd jobs than other activities. These differences tied to socio-economic background, however, need to be taken with caution. Given the few subjects who are highly educated or employed in this sample, differences are not

8.2 Housework Among Elder Adults

Table 8.3 Multiple regression models. Dependent variable: minutes spent cooking, cleaning and washing, and doing odd jobs. Women and men aged 65 and above. ISTAT TUS 2013–2014. Unweighted values. Own calculations

	Women			Men		
	Cook	Clean and wash	Odd jobs	Cook	Clean and wash	Odd jobs
Age group (r.c. 65–74)						
≥75	−18.014***	−25.026***	−23.290***	−2.842	−5.719**	−28.184***
	(2.470)	(2.912)	(1.975)	(1.870)	(1.874)	(3.573)
Life stage (r.c. Single childless)						
Single children left	4.705	1.379	−4.031	−5.541	3.890	0.408
	(3.615)	(4.261)	(2.889)	(3.805)	(3.814)	(7.272)
Couple childless	44.145***	32.966***	1.317	−42.103***	−16.643***	11.249
	(5.828)	(6.871)	(4.659)	(4.149)	(4.159)	(7.929)
Couple children left	45.958***	40.751***	−5.399	−41.194***	−11.155***	18.630**
	(3.721)	(4.387)	(2.975)	(3.165)	(3.172)	(6.048)
Level of education (r.c. Low ed.)						
Medium ed.	−16.526***	−2.414	4.080	−0.329	−2.724	−9.085
	(3.404)	(4.013)	(2.721)	(2.438)	(2.444)	(4.659)
High ed.	−28.877***	−14.997*	16.012***	−0.955	−1.816	−17.830**
	(5.253)	(6.193)	(4.199)	(3.346)	(3.354)	(6.394)
Not employed (r.c. Employed)	45.703***	33.209***	16.652*	19.804***	11.853**	26.840***
	(8.524)	(10.050)	(6.814)	(3.797)	(3.807)	(7.257)
Geographical area (r.c. North West)						
North East	−3.836	−1.027	5.776*	−4.439	1.804	7.484
	(3.421)	(4.033)	(2.735)	(2.701)	(2.708)	(5.162)

(continued)

Table 8.3 (continued)

	Women			Men		
	Cook	Clean and wash	Odd jobs	Cook	Clean and wash	Odd jobs
Centre	−5.692	−4.526	1.581	−3.711	−5.889*	3.641
	(3.459)	(4.078)	(2.765)	(2.792)	(2.799)	(5.335)
South	0.997	7.336	−5.580*	−13.318***	−10.080***	−3.283
	(3.259)	(3.842)	(2.605)	(2.589)	(2.595)	(4.947)
Islands	−5.019	6.269	−3.847	−7.454*	−8.095*	14.835*
	(4.424)	(5.216)	(3.537)	(3.626)	(3.635)	(6.930)
Week day (r.c. Weekend)	3.677	17.536***	11.145***	−0.105	2.756	24.168***
	(2.406)	(2.837)	(1.923)	(1.941)	(1.946)	(3.709)
Constant	69.710***	64.925***	35.857***	58.799***	30.661***	43.650***
	(9.232)	(10.884)	(7.380)	(4.999)	(5.011)	(9.553)
N	4323	4323	4323	3185	3185	3185
Significance	0.000	0.000	0.000	0.000	0.000	0.000

Note r.c. = reference category. *p<0.05, **p<0.01, ***p<0.001

necessarily meaningful in substantial terms. Another interesting finding lies in geographical differences: in contrast to the findings for the age groups discussed in other chapters, we can see no significant differences among women in the five areas. Thus, the cultural differences previously discussed do not seem to apply to women above a certain age. For example, on average and all other things equal, women spend about 125 min cooking, regardless of area of residence. Significant differences emerge instead for men, who spend the smallest amount of all in the South (30 min) and the largest in the North West (45 min). To further explore gender differences in housework in this age group, we now move to the analyses of the division of chores among partners.

8.3 Division of Domestic Work Among Older Adults

Table 8.4 reports descriptive figures indicating to what extent elderly couples share housework. If we focus on the general component, it appears that women do about 74% of the workload. However, the table reveals that most of men's contribution comes from odd jobs, where men contribute about 60%. If we look at cooking and cleaning, it becomes evident that women do much more: about 85% of the cooking and the washing and cleaning. Thus, once again we can observe an evident task specialization, with women being much more engaged in the routine and time-inflexible tasks and men in the (likely) more pleasurable ones (Poortman and Van der Lippe 2009).

Table 8.5 reports the results for the multivariate analyses of couples' division of chores. As can be seen, most of the variables included in the models are not statistically significant, with few exceptions. Elder women seem to do relatively less, and men somewhat more, but the coefficients are very small and not always statistically significant. Life course stage, marital status, level of education of the respondents and their partners do not affect the division of domestic chores.

Table 8.4 Average share of different housework activities (%). Partnered women and men aged 65 and above. ISTAT TUS 2013–2014. Unweighted values. Own calculations

	Housework	Cooking	Cleaning and washing	Odd jobs
	Men			
Childless	25.34	14.90	13.66	58.39
N	299	291	280	232
Children left	27.40	15.80	14.28	61.81
N	2027	1994	1919	1625
	Women			
Childless	75.35	85.44	87.32	44.07
N	231	224	215	182
Children left	73.08	84.20	86	38.44
N	1648	1619	1565	1314

Table 8.5 Multiple generalized linear models. Dependent variable: partners' share of cooking, cleaning and washing, and doing odd jobs. Coupled women and men aged 65 and above. ISTAT TUS 2013–2014. Unweighted values. Own calculations

	Women			Men		
	Cook	Clean and wash	Odd jobs	Cook	Clean and wash	Odd jobs
Age group (r.c. 65–74)						
≥75	−0.286*	−0.226	−0.197+	0.108	−0.040	−0.071
	(0.136)	(0.144)	(0.117)	(0.119)	(0.126)	(0.099)
Couples child-out	−0.174	−0.125	−0.208	0.157	0.095	0.156
	(0.204)	(0.220)	(0.163)	(0.178)	(0.188)	(0.145)
Not married (r.c. Married)	−0.323	0.139	0.030	0.491	0.012	0.351
	(0.432)	(0.550)	(0.387)	(0.355)	(0.439)	(0.348)
Level of education (r.c. Low ed.)						
Medium ed.	−0.247	−0.092	0.125	0.254	−0.021	−0.122
	(0.201)	(0.224)	(0.173)	(0.166)	(0.183)	(0.142)
High ed.	−0.205	−0.170	0.255	0.272	0.164	−0.248
	(0.340)	(0.386)	(0.283)	(0.252)	(0.276)	(0.217)
Partner's level of education (r.c. Low ed.)						
Medium ed.	−0.259	0.117	0.034	0.246	−0.029	−0.000
	(0.188)	(0.211)	(0.159)	(0.176)	(0.196)	(0.155)
High ed.	−0.206	0.042	0.222	0.187	0.196	−0.374
	(0.288)	(0.327)	(0.242)	(0.286)	(0.308)	(0.244)
Not employed (r.c. Employed)	0.298	0.076	0.239	0.588*	0.503+	0.695***
	(0.406)	(0.484)	(0.418)	(0.288)	(0.299)	(0.206)
Geographical area (r.c. North West)						
North East	0.171	−0.062	−0.093	−0.119	0.065	0.161
	(0.185)	(0.193)	(0.156)	(0.165)	(0.172)	(0.142)
Centre	0.118	0.076	0.102	−0.134	−0.072	−0.068
	(0.187)	(0.202)	(0.157)	(0.171)	(0.183)	(0.145)
South	0.477*	0.442*	−0.058	−0.497**	−0.467*	0.079
	(0.190)	(0.204)	(0.154)	(0.170)	(0.182)	(0.138)
Islands	0.209	0.383	−0.264	−0.157	−0.239	0.369+
	(0.262)	(0.298)	(0.221)	(0.228)	(0.249)	(0.196)
Relative income (r.c. Same income)						
Income > partner	−0.213	−0.397	0.327	−0.192	−0.015	−0.003
	(0.278)	(0.306)	(0.252)	(0.126)	(0.135)	(0.106)
Income < partner	0.105	−0.095	0.052	0.183	0.215	−0.419*
	(0.141)	(0.153)	(0.118)	(0.223)	(0.243)	(0.200)
Week day (r.c. weekend)	0.159	0.168	0.060	−0.035	−0.002	−0.106
	(0.140)	(0.150)	(0.111)	(0.124)	(0.130)	(0.100)

(continued)

8.3 Division of Domestic Work Among Older Adults

Table 8.5 (continued)

	Women			Men		
	Cook	Clean and wash	Odd jobs	Cook	Clean and wash	Odd jobs
Constant	1.488**	1.843***	−0.533	−2.275***	−2.235***	−0.234
	(0.463)	(0.541)	(0.457)	(0.356)	(0.374)	(0.271)
N	1843	1780	1496	2285	2199	1857
Significance	0.000	0.000	0.000	0.000	0.000	0.000

Note r.c. = reference category. $^+p<0.10$, $*p<0.05$, $**p<0.01$, $***p<0.001$

Employment status has a positive effect but only among men. Area of residence, instead, significantly affects the division of chores among elderly adults, with women doing relatively more and men relatively less cooking and washing and cleaning in the South than in the other regions. For example, on average, men in the South do 11% of the cooking against nearly 18% in the North West. For women, the figures are respectively 88 and 82%. The values for washing and cleaning follow the same pattern. Hence, the results indicate that the division of domestic chores among older adults is mostly un-affected by personal and household characteristics, expect for area of residence.

8.4 Adult Care in the Empty Nest

The final aspect we consider is adult care among elder women and men. Considering the average age of the subjects, it is mainly during this life course stage that we expect women and, less so, men to be involved in the care of aging parents and spouses. Table 8.6 reports three types of information by gender and stage of the life course: the average minutes spent on adult care; the percentage of subjects who engaged in the activity on the diary day; and the average minutes spent by those who engaged in this activity. First of all, it can be noticed that average minutes on adult care as well as percentages of engaged subjects are very low, thus suggesting that even in this age group, time spent caring for other adults is relatively little. As noted previously, time use data is not the most suited to study adult care, as it is an activity that involves a minority of subjects. Since data is collected on a single day, the risk of underestimating care activities is rather high. The values for those who engaged in adult care, however, suggest that it is a rather time-consuming activity. The few childless women and men who engaged in adult care on the diary day logged a considerable number of minutes, and the time is also quite high among coupled adults whose children left the home and among parents whose children still live at home.

Table 8.6 Summary statistics for adult care. Coupled men and women aged 65 and above. ISTAT TUS 2013–2014. Unweighted values. Own calculations

	Men	Women
Childless		
Min.	3.77 (N 313)	7.98 (N 238)
%	2.88	7.98
Min. – doers	131	100
Children left		
Min.	3.48 (N 2096)	6.88 (N 1692)
%	4.34	8.75
Min. – doers	80	78
Parents		
Min.	5.13 (N 741)	9.98 (N 426)
%	4.72	11.74
Min. – doers	108	85

8.5 Conclusions

This chapter has focused on adult women and men in the so-called empty nest phase, that is, ages 65 and above. Specifically, the chapter has looked at the allocation of time on and participation in housework among single and coupled women and men who are either childless or whose children have left the parental home. The chapter has also provided a description of the division of domestic chores among older partners and on the allocation of time to adult care. The results have revealed interesting insights about this age group. First and foremost, we show that even in this stage women spend more time on domestic chores than men. However, in line with specialization theories, larger gender gaps are observed among coupled women and men than among singles. Furthermore, the findings indicate that few individual characteristics beyond gender and life course stage are useful in predicting housework time in this age group. Among these, the level of education and employment status are the most relevant. The results also show a division of domestic labour that is far from equal, pointing to relatively larger contributions from men in odd jobs than in the routine day-by-day activities such as cooking, cleaning and washing. Moreover, individual and household variables have little effect in predicting the share of domestic tasks. One variable, however, matters for time on housework, and that is age. Indeed, the models for absolute time showed that older women and men spend decreasing amounts of time on domestic chores.

To better illustrate this pattern, Fig. 8.2 plots time on the different components of housework among increasingly old subjects.[1] As can be seen, the gender gap in housework time decreases progressively as women and men age, to the point that gender differences virtually disappear among the oldest subjects. Focusing on

---

[1]Figure 8.2 is based on data from the 2008–2009 wave as in such dataset the exact age is available for each respondent, whereas in the 2013–2014 release age is top coded at 75 years old.

8.5 Conclusions

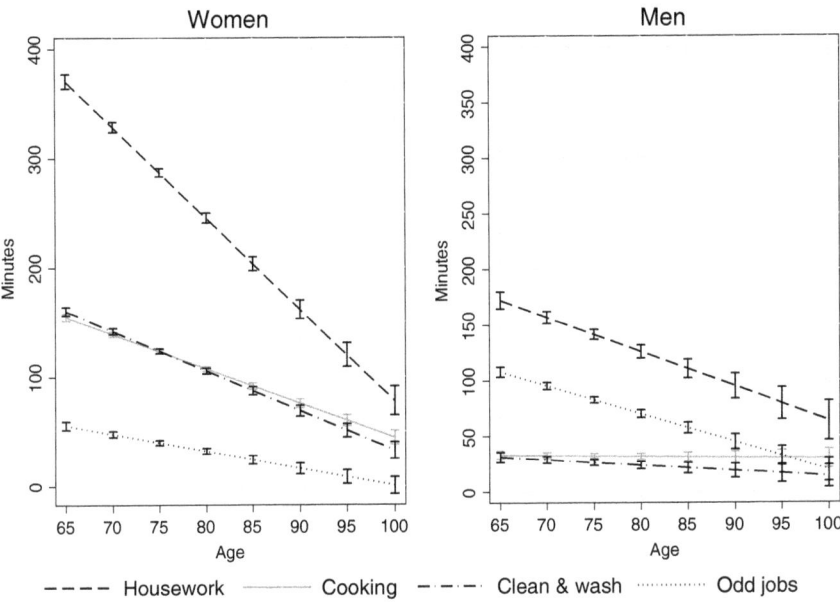

Fig. 8.2 Predicted minutes of housework and 95% confidence intervals among women and men aged 65 and above. ISTAT TUS 2008–2009. Own calculations

general housework, the figure clearly shows a large gap between women and men around age 65, as women average over 350 min per day and men less than 200. Among the older subjects, women's time decreases to less than 100 min per day. Of course, relatively few women reach this age and therefore the value is subject to statistical uncertainty, but the figure is nonetheless remarkably high. Men's time also decreases to about 50 min among the older subjects. However, the decline is mostly driven by reductions in odd jobs. In contrast, the decrease for women is driven by reductions in all types of housework.

Finally, the chapter engaged in a description of adult care time and participation. Our results revealed that only few women and men in this age group spend time on adult care. As shown in other chapters, however, those who do engage in adult care spend relatively long stretches of time on this activity. Moreover, the findings showed that there are only marginal differences between women and men, suggesting that variables other than gender matter in the allocation of time to adult care. Indeed, previous studies revealed that elements such as kinship and geographical residence are very important to understand adult care time (Barnett 2013; Henz 2006; Szinovacz and Davey 2008). As mentioned, these aspects cannot be kept into account with the current data.

In the next and last chapter, we draw some general conclusions on domestic time in Italy and take a final look at the time use data to explore historical changes in housework and childcare. Moreover, the chapter provides some insights into

Italians' attitudes toward gender roles and their satisfaction with the way chores are shared between partners.

References

Barnett, A. E. (2013). Pathways of adult children providing care to older parents. *Journal of Marriage and Family, 75*(1), 178–190.
Blood, R., & Wolfe, D. (1960). *Husbands and wives: The dynamics of married living*. New York, NY: Free Press.
Brines, J. (1994). Economic dependency, gender, and the division of labor at home. *American Journal of Sociology, 100*(3), 652–688.
Chesley, N., & Poppie, K. (2009). Assisting parents and in-laws: Gender, type of assistance, and couples' employment. *Journal of Marriage and Family, 71*(2), 247–262.
Eurostat (2017a) Employment, main characteristics and rates. Annual averages. Retrieved July 7, 2017, from http://appsso.eurostat.ec.europa.eu/nui/submitViewTableAction.do.
Eurostat (2017b) Population by educational attainment level, sex and age (%)—main indicators. Retrieved August 1, 2017, from http://appsso.eurostat.ec.europa.eu/nui/show.do?dataset=edat_lfse_03&lang=en.
Henz, U. (2006). Informal caregiving at working age: Effects of job characteristics and family configuration. *Journal of Marriage and Family, 68*(2), 411–429.
Henz, U. (2009). Couples' provision of informal care for parents and parents-in-law: far from sharing equally? *Ageing & Society, 29*(03), 369–395.
Henz, U. (2010). Parent care as unpaid family labor: How do spouses share? *Journal of Marriage and Family, 72*(1), 148–164.
Poortman, A. R., & Van der Lippe, T. (2009). Attitudes toward housework and child care and the gendered division of labor. *Journal of Marriage and Family, 71*(3), 526–541.
Sarkisian, N., & Gerstel, N. (2004). Explaining the gender gap in help to parents: The importance of employment. *Journal of Marriage and Family, 66*(2), 431–451.
Szinovacz, M. E., & Davey, A. (2008). The division of parent care between spouses. *Ageing & Society, 28*(04), 571–597.

Chapter 9
Conclusions

Abstract This chapter offers a chapter-by-chapter overview of the main results of the volume and then exploits the repeated waves of the Italian Time Use Survey to give a descriptive overview of how time in the domestic setting has changed from the first wave in 1988–89 to the most recent wave in 2013–14. The results confirm previous studies by showing that, over the decades, women have been spending less time on housework and men more, thus resulting in an overall more gender-equal division of domestic chores among partners. Moreover, childcare time has also increased over the years, in line with previous international literature. The chapter draws on the results to discuss the implications of inequalities in domestic time for societal gender inequality and suggests avenues for future research.

Keywords Domestic work · Housework · Childcare · Adult care
Life course · Italy · Italian time use survey · Gender inequality
Changes over time

9.1 Time Use in the Domestic Setting in Italy: Essential Facts and Figures

This volume has addressed gender inequalities in domestic work over the life course in Italy, a country that is renowned for its overall low levels of gender equality in the private and public fields (Anxo et al. 2011; Dotti Sani 2012; EIGE 2015; Eurostat 2017; WEF 2016). By analysing recent and detailed time use data covering over 40,000 individuals, the book has shed much needed light on the distinctive features of housework, childcare and adult care among Italian women and men from childhood to their later years. The empirical chapters of the volume focused on individuals in five different stages of the life course: children living in the parental home, childless women and men, parents of children aged 14 or younger, parents of children aged 15 or older, and adults aged 65 and above. The results highlighted that gender inequalities in the domestic sphere are present and evident in nearly every moment of women's and men's lives.

© The Author(s) 2018
G. M. Dotti Sani, *Time Use in Domestic Settings Throughout the Life Course*,
SpringerBriefs in Sociology, https://doi.org/10.1007/978-3-319-78720-6_9

Starting from childhood, Chap. 4 showed that, as early as elementary school, little girls engage more in domestic work than little boys and spend more time doing chores as well. The gap continues to increase in adolescence and, by the age of 20, girls are doing over double the amount of housework to boys. Girls are also more likely to engage in typically female activities such as cooking, cleaning and doing the laundry, whereas boys are more involved in odd jobs, such as small repairs and taking out the rubbish. Chapter 4 also showed that having a father who engaged in domestic chores is a strong predictor of children's participation. This result is especially evident for boys, suggesting the existence of a gender specific pattern of imitation between fathers and sons. In other words, fathers who are involved in the care of their home act as positive role models for their sons: an encouraging starting point for long-term changes in the gendered allocation of housework. However, the general finding that girls do more housework than boys is much less inspiring, as it indicates that cultural norms on gendered behaviour have a strong impact on children.

Chapter 5 examined time spent on, and participation in, housework among childless women and men living independently or in couples. Like children, women and men at this stage were not expected to be strongly affected by dynamics of time availability, power and resources. In contrast, our results indicate that gender differences are present among singles as well as partnered individuals. In line with theories of task specialization, however, gender differences peak among couples: while about $\sim$ 75% of partnered childless men engage in general housework on the diary day, the value is down to $\sim$ 50% for cooking, $\sim$ 37% for cleaning and $\sim$ 3% for washing and doing the laundry. The figures for partnered women are, respectively, $\sim$ 95%, $\sim$ 88%, $\sim$ 75% and $\sim$ 30%. The chapter also analysed whether individual characteristics–such as level of education, employment status and area of residence—affect time on and participation in housework. The results largely confirm previous findings (Bianchi et al. 2012; Greenstein 2000): highly educated women do fewer chores than low educated women, and non-employed women do more than the employed. Moreover, women in the Southern regions and the Islands do more housework than in the North and men less, again confirming previous results on the great cultural differences within the country, which see the South as more traditional (Dotti Sani 2012). Thus, even among younger and, in principle, modern Italians, women are doing significantly more housework than men.

Chapter 6 focused on parents of children aged 14 or younger. In line with previous literature (Anxo et al. 2011; Schober 2013), the results show that domestic gender inequalities at this stage of life are extreme: virtually all mothers (99%) did at least 10 min of housework on the diary day against approximatively 75% of fathers. Differences in time spent on domestic work are even more striking, with fathers averaging about 92 min per day and mothers about 280. The findings also show that mothers spend more time taking care of their children than fathers. However, mothers are mostly responsible for physical care and helping with homework, whereas fathers are mostly involved in interactive care. Finally, the chapter engaged in the analysis of

9.1 Time Use in the Domestic Setting in Italy: Essential Facts and Figures

adult care, revealing that it is a rather uncommon activity characterized by minor gender differences.

In Chap. 7, the focus shifted to parents of children aged 15 and older. The chapter also included a comparison with women and men aged 45 to 64 who are childless or whose children have left the parental home. We analyse parents of older children in a separate chapter because, while the number of chores and time constraints generated by the presence of young children should gradually decrease over time, more time might be needed for the care of aging adults. The chapter illustrated that gender and household status account for great differences in housework time. For example, childless partnered women perform about 273 min of housework per day while childless partnered men about 119. In contrast, partnered women with children in the household spend about 340 min on housework, while men with the same household status only 118. The pattern for participation in housework is similar. As for individual characteristics, the results show that highly educated women spend less time on chores than low educated women, while education does not affect men's housework. Non-employed women and men spend more time on housework than their employed counterparts. Finally, living in the South is associated with doing more housework for women and less for men. The chapter also revealed that relatively little time is spent caring for other adults, despite our expectation of greater time investment in adult care among these subjects.

Lastly, Chap. 8 considered the allocation of time to housework among women and men aged 65 and above. Similar to Chap. 7, we find that gender differences in housework time are greatest among couples and smallest among singles, pointing to long-lasting effects of task specialization. Education and employment status are also rather strong predictors of housework time among these older Italians, while area of residence accounts for some of the time spent on chores by men. Age is also an important predictor of housework time: among the oldest of the old, gender differences in housework time virtually disappear. Average minutes spent on adult care as well as percentages of engaged subjects are very low, as was found for other groups considered in the book. This result reinforces the notion that time use data are not apt for the study of adult care. However, the values for those who engaged in adult care indicate how time consuming the activity is and point to the importance of external help in this respect.

Overall, the results presented in the volume indicate that time spent on and participation in domestic work is very far from being gender equal, as women are more involved in domestic work than men at all ages. Gender inequalities in housework are smallest among very young children and greatest among parents. Within this group, inequalities also emerge when it comes to childcare. Not only do mothers engage in more childcare than fathers: they also engage more in the routine and least enjoyable tasks, whereas fathers engage more in the most pleasurable ones. Therefore, differences emerge not just in terms of quantity but also of quality.

To get a general and conclusive idea about gender inequalities in the distribution of domestic chores in Italy, Fig. 9.1 shows the average minutes spent on housework by women and men at each stage of the life course. Beyond the fact that at virtually all ages women spend more time on domestic chores than men, the figure shows that age and household status are also highly relevant. For example, a mother aged 20–34 does considerably more chores than a childless partnered woman (263 min/day vs. 208 min/day), and even more than a childless single woman in the same age group (137 min/day).

Age also has a positive effect among men, but the effect of household status is much smaller. For example, a father aged 20 to 34 does about 84 min/day of housework, a childless partnered man about 94, and a childless single man again about 84. Task specialization in this respect is revealed by the fact that single women do fewer chores than partnered ones, while single men on average spend more time on domestic work than their partnered peers.

Figure 9.2 shows a different side of the story by reporting the curvilinear effect of age on the time spent on housework by women and men.[1] Women and men spend similar amounts of time on housework only when they are very young, or very old. For example, boys and girls below age 10 spend about 16 and 19 min on chores per day respectively, with only a 3 min difference. The difference is also relatively small among the oldest adults: at age 90 and above, women spend nearly 100 min on chores and men about 56. The gender gap is widest at the central stages of life: women in their thirties and forties, respectively, outdo men by 165 and 207 min of housework. However, it is between 50 and 60 years old that the gender gap peaks. This difference—that amounts to nearly three hours—excludes caring activities, which can be quite time consuming and cumbersome as shown in the previous chapters. The gap then starts to diminish but, as mentioned, never completely disappears.

9.2 Traditional Behaviours, Traditional Attitudes?

What are the potential consequences of gender inequality in time use? Beyond general considerations regarding the importance of equality per se between women and men in the private and public fields, several authors have documented the problematic consequences of the lack of balance of chores within households. Indeed, too much housework leads to lower wages (Bryan and Sevilla-Sanz 2011) and decreased fertility (Miettinen et al. 2015; Mills et al. 2008). Moreover, an excess of housework is associated with lower levels of happiness (Mencarini and Sironi 2010). However, recent research on Italy suggests that, despite being overburdened by the second shift (Hochschild 1989), Italian women are generally satisfied with their allocation of time to unpaid work (Carriero and Todesco 2016). Does this apply to the women considered in this volume? Figure 9.3 shows the percentages of coupled women and men in the sample that are completely satisfied, satisfied, dissatisfied and completely dissatisfied with the way they share housework with their partner. The modal category

---

[1] Figure 9.2 is based on data from the 2008–2009 wave of the Italian Time Use Survey, when detailed age information was released also for women and men age 75 and above.

9.2 Traditional Behaviours, Traditional Attitudes?

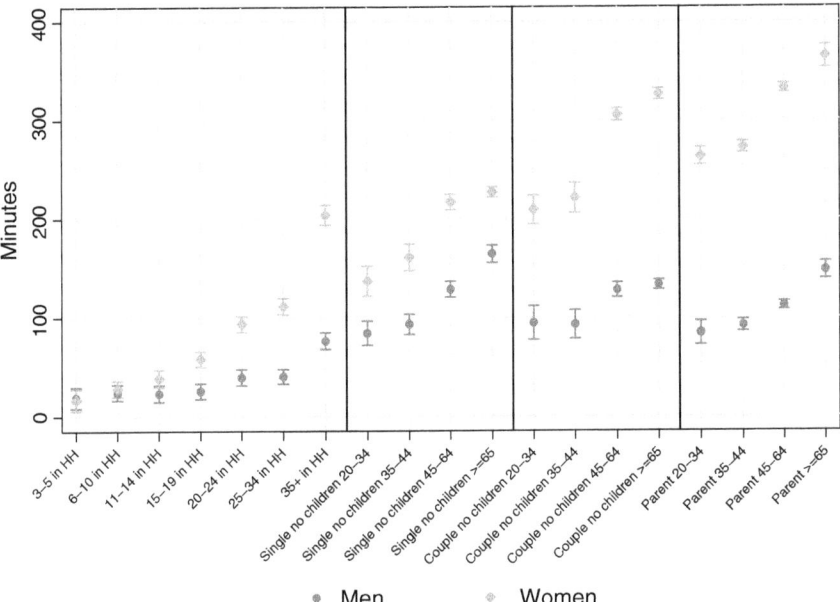

Fig. 9.1 Predicted minutes of housework with 95% confidence intervals by stage of the life course and gender. ISTAT TUS 2013–2014. Own calculations

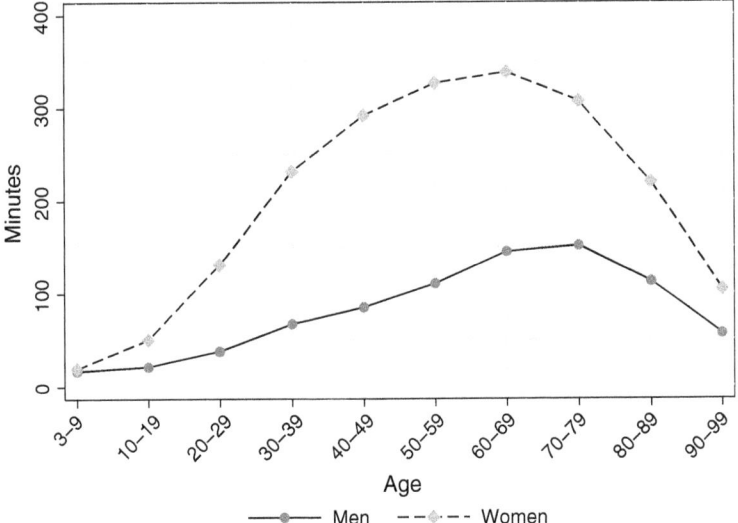

Fig. 9.2 Average minutes of housework by age and gender. ISTAT TUS 2008–2009. Unweighted values. Own calculations

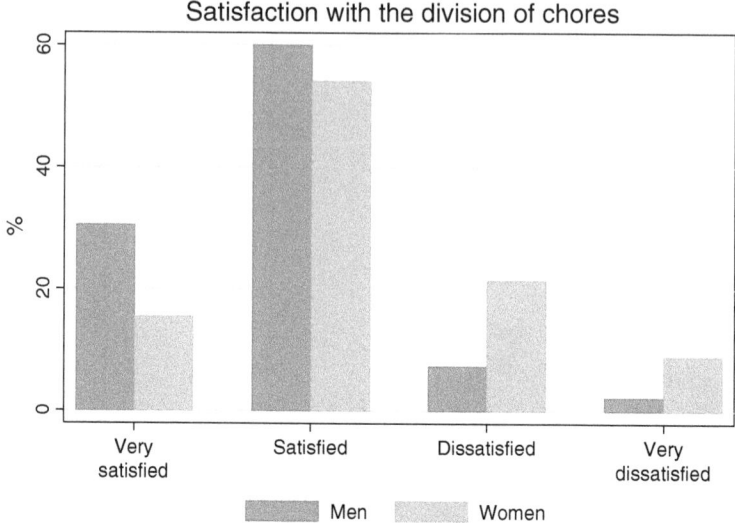

Fig. 9.3 Satisfaction with the division of housework expressed as percentage by gender. Coupled women and men. ISTAT TUS 2013–2014. Unweighted values. Own calculations

for both genders is being satisfied, with men being somewhat more likely to fall into this category than women (60% vs. 54%). Moreover, men are twice as likely as women to declare being completely satisfied (30% vs. 15%). Conversely, women are more likely to be dissatisfied (21%) and completely dissatisfied (9%) than men (7% and 2% respectively). Thus, it appears that overall men are considerably more satisfied than women about the division of domestic chores, with men's distribution being more skewed to the left than women's.

Considering that women do the lion's share of the domestic work, it is somewhat surprising that they are mostly satisfied with the division of housework. Italians, however, are known for having fairly traditional views concerning women's and men's roles in society, a fact that could partly explain this finding. To explore this issue, we report in Table 9.1 the results of a battery of questions about attitudes towards gender roles that coupled women and men in the sample were asked. When asked whether "it is best for the family if the man works and the woman takes care of the home", the modal category is agreement for both men (37%) and women (34%). A full 25% of men disagree with the statement "If both partners work full-time, the man must do the same amount of chores as the woman" while nearly 30% of women completely agree. Couples are more inclined to agree about having an equal division of childcare: women and men similarly agree that parents should take turns taking care of a sick child ($\sim$45%) and that fathers are competent caregivers ($\sim$40%). The feelings about competence in domestic work, however, are quite different, as both women and men disagree with the notion that "Men are just as competent as women in doing domestic chores" (modal category 37%). Finally, women are more likely to completely agree with the statement "It is important that

9.2 Traditional Behaviours, Traditional Attitudes?

Table 9.1 Attitudes toward gender and family roles (%). Coupled men and women (N 19868). ISTAT TUS 2013–2014. Unweighted values. Own calculations

	Completely Agree		Agree		Disagree		Completely Disagree	
	M	W	M	W	M	W	M	W
It is best for the family if the man works and the woman takes care of the home	19	13	37	34	24	25	20	28
If both partners work full-time, the man must do the same amount of chores as the woman	19	27	48	49	25	19	8	5
Men are just as competent as women in doing domestic chores	12	11	33	31	37	37	18	21
If both parents work full-time and a child is sick, parents must take turns caring for the child	32	36	46	45	16	14	6	5
Fathers are just as competent as mothers in taking care of young children	16	17	40	41	33	31	10	11
It is important that the home be always clean and tidy	44	54	48	41	7	4	1	1

Note M = Men. W = Women

the home be always clean and tidy." Thus, it seems that the unequal division of domestic work in Italian households is underpinned and accompanied by relatively traditional attitudes toward gender roles.

9.3 Changing Times: Historical Changes in Housework and Childcare

One last piece of information that can be drawn from the Italian Time Use Survey regards how housework and childcare time have changed over the years. Pooling information from the four waves of data (1988–89, 2002–03, 2008–09, 2013–14),

Fig. 9.4 shows variations in housework time among Italian couples aged 20–64 over time. As can be seen from the panel on the left, women have considerably decreased their time on cooking and washing the dishes, while time on the residual odd job category has increased. Time spent washing and cleaning the house has remained rather stable over the period. The panel on the right reports the results for men, and shows substantial increases in all three groups of activities, despite odd jobs being the area where Italian men still invest the greatest amounts of time.

In line with these results, Fig. 9.5 shows that over the decades the share of overall housework has become more gender equal, with women doing relatively less, and men relative more. As shown by the solid grey line, women's share of housework in 1988–89 was about 86% and men's 13%. By 2002–03, we observe a sharp decline and the values become 79% and 20% respectively, remaining fairly stable in the following wave. In 2013–14 we observe a further move toward an egalitarian division of labour, with women doing 75% and men 25%. Thus, over the period in question, partnered men have gone from doing less than one sixth to about one fourth of the overall domestic workload. The division of cooking as well as washing and cleaning has also become more equal, with women doing over 90% of these activities in 1988–89 to about 85% in 2013–14. The relative time partners spend on odd jobs has also become more gender equal, as women engage progressively more and men progressively less in this group of tasks. In this respect, Italians seem to be following a more general, global trend that sees men progressively more involved in the domestic sphere than in the past (Bianchi 2011; Bianchi et al. 2000, 2012; Gershuny 2000; Sayer et al. 2004). The values presented here are calculated on the entire sample of couples, therefore compositional changes

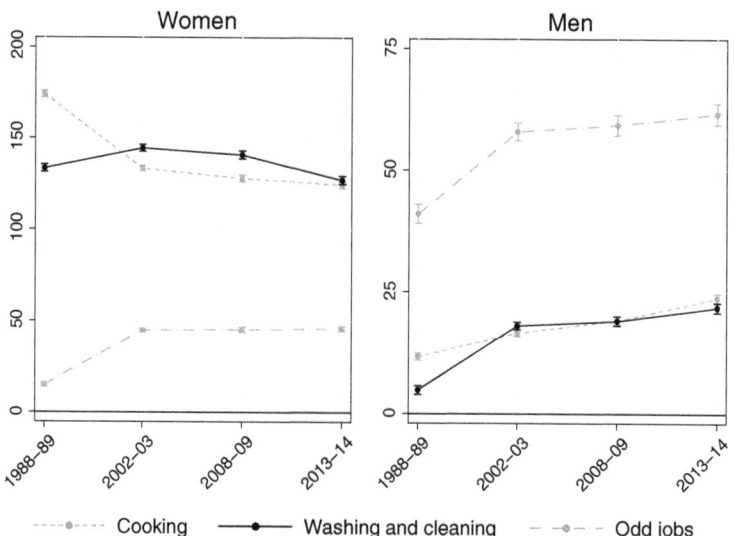

Fig. 9.4 Predicted minutes with 95% confidence intervals for cooking, washing and cleaning, and doing odd jobs among coupled women and men aged 20 to 64. ISTAT TUS 1988–89, 2002–03, 2008–09, 2013–14. Unweighted values. Own calculations

9.3 Changing Times: Historical Changes in Housework and Childcare

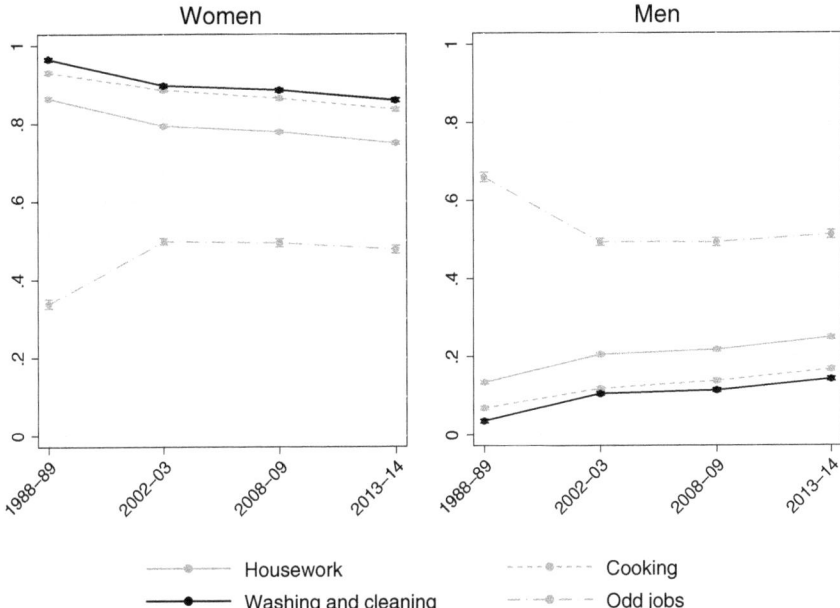

Fig. 9.5 Predicted proportion of domestic chores and 95% confidence intervals for coupled women and men aged 20 to 64. ISTAT TUS 1988–89, 2002–03, 2008–09, 2013–14. Own calculations

especially in terms of female employment could be partially responsible for the declining time on housework among women. However, increases in men's housework time as well as different trends in the sub-components of housework among women suggest that changes in housework behaviour might not be exclusively the result of changing demographics.

Time spent caring for children has also changed over the decades. In line with previous studies, Italian parents have increased the amount of time spent with their children (Craig and Mullan 2011; Dotti Sani and Treas 2016; Gauthier et al. 2004). As shown in Fig. 9.6, mothers have gone from spending 43 min per day on overall childcare in 1988–89 to 57 min in 2013–14, while fathers have gone from 16 to 33 min. Interestingly, while overall care time has increased for both genders, there are notable differences in the subcomponents of childcare. In fact, mothers' time on physical care has only marginally increased from 31 to 36 min, while interactive care (that is, playing with children, reading to them and helping them with homework) has increased twice as much. Among fathers, the increase in interactive care is comparable to mothers' (from about 10 to 20 min over the period), but the increase in physical care is remarkable: it has nearly tripled, going from 5 to 14 min. However, even in the light of these changes, mothers are still spending considerably more time with their children than fathers.

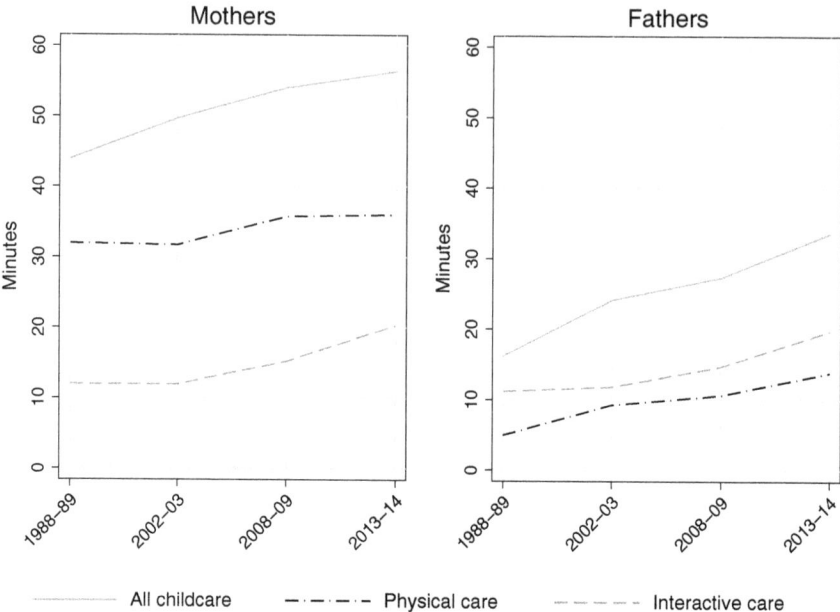

Fig. 9.6 Average minutes of all, interactive and physical childcare among coupled mothers and fathers aged 20 to 64. ISTAT TUS 1988–89, 2002–03, 2008–09, 2013–14. Unweighted values. Own calculations

9.4 Concluding Remarks

Beyond some positive signs of change in the allocation of time to unpaid work over the past decades, the analyses carried out in this volume suggest that there is little room for optimism regarding equality in the domestic field in Italy. In this respect, women and men together would benefit from policy packages favouring greater gender equality in the private sphere. For example, research has shown that an early involvement of fathers in the care of their new-borns leads to greater involvement in their children's lives later on (Grunow and Evertsson 2016), improved socio-emotional behaviour and early skills among children (Bronte-Tinkew et al. 2008; Cabrera et al. 2007; McMunn et al. 2017) and increased chances of having other children (Aassve et al. 2015; Duvander and Andersson 2006). As of 2017, however, paternity leave is restricted to just a few days and the replacement rate for parental leave is only 30% of the previous wage, therefore making it an unrealistic option for fathers who are the main breadwinners in the household.

Beyond policy drawbacks, there are several other aspects of the Italian public arena that make it an unfriendly place for women. Research has shown that women are more likely to be involved in the public and political fields in countries where women have greater political representation (Fraile and Gomez 2017; Wolbrecht and Campbell 2007). Unsurprisingly, Italy is one of the largest European countries never to have had a woman in a position of power, unlike, for example, Sweden, the United Kingdom and recently Germany. Not only are women underrepresented among Italian politicians,

9.4 Concluding Remarks

those who do occupy positions of power are often the target of misogynist comments that go well beyond acceptable criticism of public figures. Italy is also a country where, every year, many women are victims of abuse by male members of their family such as husbands, partners, fathers and brothers. According to ISTAT, in 2014 over 31% of women aged 16–70 have been physically or sexually abused by a man (ISTAT 2014) and, too often for any standard, the abuse ends up in murder (ISTAT 2017). Thus, beyond what the volume has shown about inequality in the domestic sphere, there is still much to improve in the social standing of Italian women.

An important task for social scientists in this respect is to increasingly monitor women's position by adopting comprehensive approaches to study the inequalities women face in the public and private fields. Political underrepresentation, occupational segregation, pay gaps, glass ceilings and sticky floors, along with inequalities in unpaid domestic work are all aspects of the same problem and need to be jointly taken into account to thoroughly address gender inequalities. Moreover, research must further pursue the study of the making of gender inequalities. Greater emphasis must be placed on the early development of gendered behaviours and preferences, and on the subtle transition that individuals make from being "blank slates" to holders of clear-cut attitudes towards gender roles. Although this transition has been shown to occur at an early age, we need more cross-national and longitudinal research in this area. Considering the great differences in terms of attitudes toward gender roles that are displayed by adults with different socio-cultural backgrounds (Baxter and Kane 1995; Edlund and Öun 2016), it is crucial to tease out the intervening factors that occur during childhood that make some adults become more gender egalitarian than others.

References

Aassve, A., Fuochi, G., Mencarini, L., & Mendola, D. (2015). What is your couple type? Gender ideology, housework sharing, and babies. *Demographic Research, 32*(30), 835–858.

Anxo, D., Mencarini, L., Pailhé, A., Solaz, A., et al. (2011). Gender differences in time use over the life course in France, Italy, Sweden, and the US. *Feminist Economics, 17*(3), 159–195.

Baxter, J., & Kane, E. W. (1995). Dependence and independence: A cross-national analysis of gender inequality and gender attitudes. *Gender & Society, 9*(2), 193–215.

Bianchi, S., Milkie, M., Sayer, L., & Robinson, J. (2000). Is anyone doing the housework? Trends in the gender division of household labor. *Social Forces, 79*(1), 191–228.

Bianchi, S. M. (2011). Family change and time allocation in American families. *The ANNALS of the American Academy of Political and Social Science, 638*(1), 21–44.

Bianchi, S. M., Sayer, L. C., Milkie, M. A., & Robinson, J. P. (2012). Housework: Who did, does or will do it, and how much does it matter? *Social Forces, 91*(1), 55–63.

Bronte-Tinkew, J., Carrano, J., Horowitz, A., & Kinukawa, A. (2008). Involvement among resident fathers and links to infant cognitive outcomes. *Journal of Family Issues, 29*(9), 1211–1244.

Bryan, M. L., & Sevilla-Sanz, A. (2011). Does housework lower wages? Evidence for Britain. *Oxford Economic Papers, 63*(1), 187–210.

Cabrera, N. J., Shannon, J. D., & Tamis-LeMonda, C. (2007). Fathers' influence on their children's cognitive and emotional development: From toddlers to Pre-K. *Applied Developmental Science, 11*(4), 208–213.

Carriero, R., & Todesco, L. (2016). *Indaffarate e soddisfatte. Donne, uomini e lavoro familiare in Italia*. Rome: Carocci Editore.

Craig, L., & Mullan, K. (2011). How mothers and fathers share childcare a cross-national time-use comparison. *American Sociological Review, 76*(6), 834–861.

Dotti Sani, G. M. (2012). La divisione del lavoro domestico e delle attività di cura nelle coppie italiane: un'analisi empirica. *Stato e Mercato, 94*(1), 161–192.

Dotti Sani, G. M., & Treas, J. (2016). Educational gradients in parents' child-care time across countries, 1965–2012. *Journal of Marriage and Family, 78*(4), 1083–1096.

Duvander, A.-Z., & Andersson, G. (2006). Gender equality and fertility in Sweden: A study on the impact of the father's uptake of parental leave on continued childbearing. *Marriage & Family Review, 39*(1–2), 121–142.

Edlund, J., & Öun, I. (2016). Who should work and who should care? Attitudes towards the desirable division of labour between mothers and fathers in five European countries. *Acta Sociologica, 59*(2), 151–169.

EIGE (2015) Gender equality index 2015. *European Institute for Gender Equality*. www.eige.europa.eu/gender-statistics.

Eurostat (2017) Employment, main characteristics and rates. Annual averages. Retrieved July, 7 2017, from http://appsso.eurostat.ec.europa.eu/nui/submitViewTableAction.do.

Fraile, M., & Gomez, R. (2017). Bridging the enduring gender gap in political interest in Europe: The relevance of promoting gender equality. *European Journal of Political Research, 56*(3), 601–618.

Gauthier, A. H., Smeeding, T. M., & Furstenberg, F. F. (2004). Are parents investing less time in children? Trends in selected industrialized countries. *Population and Development Review, 30*(4), 647–672.

Gershuny, J. (2000). *Changing times: Work and leisure in postindustrial society*. Oxford: Oxford University Press.

Greenstein, T. N. (2000). Economic dependence, gender, and the division of labor in the home: A replication and extension. *Journal of Marriage and Family, 62*(2), 322–335.

Grunow, D., & Evertsson, M. (2016). *Couples' Transitions to Parenthood*. Cheltenham, UK Northampton, MA, USA: Edward Elgar.

Hochschild, A. (1989). *The second shift: Working parents and the revolution at home*. New York, NY: Viking.

ISTAT (2014) *La violenza contro le donne dentro e fuori la famiglia*. Presidenza del Consiglio dei Ministri e Dipartimento delle Pari Opportunità. https://www.istat.it/it/archivio/violenza.

ISTAT (2017) *Omicidi di donne*. Retrieved Feburary 8, 2018, from https://www.istat.it/it/violenza-sulle-donne/il-fenomeno/omicidi-di-donne.

McMunn, A., Martin, P., Kelly, Y., & Sacker, A. (2017). Fathers' involvement: correlates and consequences for child socioemotional behavior in the United Kingdom. *Journal of Family Issues, 38*(8), 1109–1131.

Mencarini, L., & Sironi, M. (2010). Happiness, housework and gender inequality in Europe. *European Sociological Review, 28*(2), 203–219.

Miettinen, A., Lainiala, L., & Rotkirch, A. (2015). Women's housework decreases fertility: Evidence from a longitudinal study among Finnish couples. *Acta Sociologica, 58*(2), 139–154.

Mills, M., Begall, K., Mencarini, L., & Tanturri, M. L. (2008). Gender equity and fertility intentions in Italy and the Netherlands. *Demographic Research, 18*(1), 1–26.

Sayer, L. C., Bianchi, S. M., & Robinson, J. P. (2004). Are parents investing less in children? Trends in mothers' and fathers' time with children. *American Journal of Sociology, 110*(1), 1–43.

Schober, P. S. (2013). The parenthood effect on gender inequality: Explaining the change in paid and domestic work when British couples become parents. *European Sociological Review, 29*(1), 74–85.

WEF (2016) *The Global Gender Gap Report*. World Economic Forum, Geneva, Switzerland. http://reports.weforum.org/global-gender-gap-report-2016.

Wolbrecht, C., & Campbell, D. E. (2007). Leading by example: Female members of parliament as political role models. *American Journal of Political Science, 51*(4), 921–939.

GPSR Compliance

The European Union's (EU) General Product Safety Regulation (GPSR) is a set of rules that requires consumer products to be safe and our obligations to ensure this.

If you have any concerns about our products, you can contact us on

ProductSafety@springernature.com

In case Publisher is established outside the EU, the EU authorized representative is:

Springer Nature Customer Service Center GmbH
Europaplatz 3
69115 Heidelberg, Germany

www.ingramcontent.com/pod-product-compliance
Ingram Content Group UK Ltd.
Pitfield, Milton Keynes, MK11 3LW, UK
UKHW021320180426

11947UKWH00015B/1351